The History of Flagellation

THE WHIP AS AN INSTRUMENT OF PUNISHMENT, TORTURE, SELF-BEATINGS, RELIGION AND EROTIC STIMULATION

By JOSEPH McCABE

HALDEMAN-JULIUS PUBLICATIONS
GIRARD, KANSAS

Printed in the United States of America

Printing Statement:

Due to the very old age and scarcity of this book,
many of the pages may be hard to read due to the
blurring of the original text, possible missing pages,
missing text and other issues beyond our control.

Because this is such an important and rare work, we
believe it is best to reproduce this book regardless of
its original condition.

Thank you for your understanding.

INTRODUCTION

A UNIQUE MANIFESTATION OF HUMAN BEHAVIOR

The subject of flagellation, or whipping, has a unique interest from the fact that the same practice has been adopted by men as a means of extinguishing and of promoting what they call lustful impulses. Between the two extremes, the ascetic who flogs himself when he feels that his sex impulse is stirring or in order to keep it inanimate and the normal man who is stimulated by the whip, there is a broad world of types and experiences that more nearly link the extremes than is generally supposed and makes the history of the practice one of the quaintest in the study of human behavior. This history may broadly be divided into three sections. To unsophisticated man the whip—in Latin *flagellum*—is simply an instrument of cruelty. We therefore find it almost exclusively used for punishment until the Roman mind, in the early decadence of the great Greek-Roman civilization, begins to perceive other aspects of it. Until the Christian era opens therefore, and in most of the world since that time, the whip, wherever it was known, was the most familiar implement for the punishment of crimes or offenses. How far the brutal use of it was in many cases motivated by a sadistic feeling we shall inquire when the facts suggest this, but for most of us there is little or no interest in the development of forms of punishment or torture, and we will not linger over that long early stretch of man's history.

A new chapter was opened when the Christian religion put sexual offenses, and even the thought of them, on the same level of misbehavior as crimes, if not on a lower level. I will recall at the proper place how we correct the traditional error that is involved in this statement. The reprobation of sex as such, and apart from marriage, began several centuries before the Christian Era, but as that era developed it took on a more complex form and the world began to learn from its teachers that the most peremptory of human urges was a diabolical impulse that must be strangled in its birth or expiated by suffering. In the minority of the race that took the Christian ethic seriously lashing by one's own hand or by others, reached a veritable fury of virtue, and the self-tormenter was as proud of the scars on his back and loins as the soldier was of the scars on his breast. The anemic and untruthful manuals of history which are now used in our schools, even in our universities, so seriously falsify the taste and standards of that age that folk are not inclined to believe how gross, from our modern angle, were the practices even of the ascetic.

Just as serious is the falsification, by suppression, of the enormously widespread hypocrisy of the Middle Ages or the general practice of being content with lip-homage to the creeds and ignoring the moral code they were suppose to enforce. The outcome of the extraordinary type of mind that was formed by this fusion of an ascetic creed with one of the most boisterous sensual lives yet seen on this planet was, in the matter of flagellation, a gallery of portraits and incidents that can hardly be equaled in any other literature. We get a few monks and nuns in all ages lashing their bodies barbarously: we get saints stripping naked noble ladies who have tempted them and scourging them until the blood flows: we get a widespread, if not common, practice of priest-confessors licking their lips as they order their fairer penitents to strip and receive the lash. We find religious writers arguing that the most graceful curves that the Creator has put upon the female form cannot have been intended as the seat of such indignity, and clerical writers desperately twisting the supposed words of Jesus, "Show thyself to the priests," into a justification of the practice of stripping lady penitents. In all this colorful mass of weird practices we shall find it impossible to disentangle the elements of sex enjoyment and sex suppression or expiation.

In modern times men begin to recognize, as some of the Romans seem to have done, that the whip is the instrument of vice as well as of virtue. We run into the strange chapter of modern works on sexual aberrations that deals with the sadist and the masochist. The whip vanishes from serious use in the churches and monasteries and makes its appearance in very different establishments, while all the time it sustains its brutal role in flogging members of what are called the lower races and in reactionary schools, jails, camps, and navies. I have had to gather the material of the story from many sources and do not present it as complete but in the absence of any substantial modern work on the subject, the reader may find it a piquant account of one of the vagaries throughout history of what we call our human nature.

CHAPTER I. FLAGELLATION IN THE ANCIENT WORLD

There is, for two reasons, little to be said about flagellation before the dawn of history or outside the range of civilization. Of what is called, by some writers on the subject, the perverse use of the whip we do not look for any trace because the primitive man neither requires any artificial stimulation of his appetites nor could dream of obtaining such stimulation by inflicting cruelty upon himself. On the other hand, he is generally amazed to find civilized folk and their missionaries finding evil in some of his natural functions while surrendering themselves to the frank and full enjoyment of others, such as eating and drinking. Interfering with another man's wife or daughter is an offense against property for which he takes the risk of tribal punishment or personal vengeance, but it is difficult for him to see any law, even in theory, beyond that. Instead in almost all cases the tribe wants children, and the idea of checking his procreativeness seems to him absurd. It is only by a backing of the armed force of his nation that the missionary can drag him from his fertility goddess to the Virgin Mary; and he often ingeniously combines the two.

But there is another reason why we find comparatively little flagellation amongst precivilized peoples and in early civilization. A missionary-anthropologist suggests that the first idea of flagellation was to drive evil spirits out of a man, and that at first the scourge was usually a bit of a thorn bush. When we reflect on the intense and universal belief in evil spirits below the level of civilization and the few instances we find of a practice of flagellation this seems to be an improbable theory. In my opinion the whip, in any form, was first made and used by horsemen, and as the far greater part of the backward peoples had no horses until civilized man introduced them, they were not familiar with the whip.

It was the theory of the ancient Greek and Roman writers that the Romans, who, apart from a peculiar practice in Sparta, were the first nation in Europe to make an excessive use of the whip, borrowed it from "the Scythians." This was a generic name for a medley of peoples, most probably Asiatic, who lived northeast of the Black Sea and were therefore just as likely to pass on probably through the intermediate barbarians (in what is now Bulgaria), the horse and the horsewhip to the Greeks and the Romans. It is generally believed that the horse was first extensively used as a domestic animal by these people of western Asia, and I suggest that it would be a natural development to cut a thong from the hide of a dead horse for use as a whip. To use it on a fellow human as well as a horse would easily occur. In point of fact, the ancient writers make the point that the whip was used in that way by the Scythians and Thracians. Even what they call the "nobles" (sons of chiefs or headmen) amongst them are said to have been severely flogged upon occasion. But we know so little about this dim world on the fringe of ancient civilization that it is waste of time to speculate upon it.

Apart from these we find comparatively little use of anything that can be called flagellation outside the area of civilization. Amongst the Melanesians, the peoples who are in the next grade above the Australians, we find a few practices which are loosely brought under that head. In New Caledonia it is said that when a chief was ill a girl—a sort of substitute or scapegoat—was whipped to drive the evil spirits away from him; which is one of the few slight grounds for the suggestion that flagellation began as an implement against evil spirits. In the Sandwich

Islands a King used to be beaten on the back with a sacred branch before he was installed in his dignity. It was probably a symbolical purification and hardly falls in the category we are discussing.

In Asia we have only claims that the Ainus used to beat a patient with certain herbs to expel sickness: that in certain parts of Malaya all the people were beaten in order to ward off a threat of the spread of smallpox: and that in Burma a woman who was believed to be possessed by an evil spirit was beaten with sticks. All that I can discover in the case of the great continent of Africa is that in many places flogging was part of the hardening of youths when they reached puberty; and as every kind of physical endurance is tried by savages at this stage of initiating youths to manhood, or preparing them for war, it has no special significance. Amongst the American Indians a few cases are reported. We read that in Brazil the Indians used to whip themselves on the genitals at the time of the new moon, and in some other places they were accustomed to beat each other severely on certain festivals which the experts connect with old fertility rites. In California they beat a man who developed paralysis in one or other organ, apparently in the belief that they were driving out an evil spirit. In Peru it was the custom for the people to beat each other with torches on certain festivals and say, "let all evil spirits depart," which suggests rather a sun-worship rite of driving away darkness by light.

These are the only instances collected by experts who have made research in that field, and they confirm the general truth that flagellation, or the serious use of a whip or scourge, is a practice of civilized peoples and lend considerable color to my suggestion that the taming of the horse for riding purposes was the chief source of the use of the lash. We are not concerned in a history of flagellation with every sort of thrashing. Probably from the beginning of the human period the stick was used for attack or punishment, and in most of the above cases the whipping is rather of a symbolical nature.

Amongst the early civilized nations the Egyptians, Persians and Spartans afford most evidence of flagellation. We have less evidence of customs in the case of the Babylonians and can say only that they do not seem to have made much use of the lash. Some of the evidence also in regard to the Egyptians is either doubtful or wrongly interpreted. Some writers give an air of great antiquity to the practice of flaggellation in Egypt by quoting from the Greek historian Herodotus (II, 60-61) how the vast crowds, which in one place he estimates at 700,000, who made the pilgrimage to Busiris for the festival of Iris and Osiris, used to beat themselves in the course of the ceremony. He is sometimes translated as saying that they beat each other, but besides that we hardly imagine hundreds of thousands of worshipers taking even ritual whips with them, his words seem to mean only that they beat their breasts at certain points in the services. He says:

After the sacrifice all, both men and women, beat themselves in honor of some god whose name a religious scruple forbids me to mention.

Thus the idea of the "mysteries" of Isis is kept up. The unnamed god is, of course, Osiris, and the spectacle or pageant was performed in the open air by the priests before these immense crowds of pilgrims. The essential part of the ritual was the burial and later recovery of Osiris's genital organ; and it may be that by the time of Herodotus (about 500 B.C.), when puritanical ideas from Persia had made some headway in Egypt, the priests were reticent in talking to Greek strangers about their cruder legends. The word the historian uses plainly means "to strike the breast," and this was in fact an Egyptian practice at funerals. They ritually joined in the mourning of Isis over the death and mutilation of Osiris. It may be remembered that the old legend was that his wicked brother Seth had slain Osiris and cut up the body, burying pieces in different regions, and Isis, sister and spouse of Osiris, quickly recovered most parts except the phallus and had to spend years in mourning in her search for this. It was a plain allegorization of the

6

original nature festival of the annual death of vegetation and the sun.

That the Egyptians did not take their religion seriously enough to scourge themselves or each other is plain from Herodotus's description of the behavior of the crowds he saw going up the river for the festival.

Men and women sailed together, vast numbers in each boat, many of the women with castanets which they strike while some of the men play pipes during the whole time of the voyage, the remainder of the passengers, male and female, singing the while and clapping with their hands. When they arrive at any of the towns on the banks of the river they approach the shore and, while some of the women continue to play and sing, others call aloud to the females of the place and load them with abuse, while a certain number dance and lift up their clothes (probably turning their backs in the usual primitive way) . . . More grape-wine is consumed during that festival than in all of the rest of the year.

Elsewhere he describes the women on a festival of Osiris dragging round the villages a statue of the god with a monstrous phallus which, with great gaiety, they worked with a cord.

Not much better is the supposed evidence from the Old Testament that the Egyptians used the lash on their Hebrew slaves. This was written long after the horse was introduced into Egypt and is not exactly history in any case. It seems to be an anachronism to represent them as flogging the builders of the pyramids. We have a life-like statue of one of the foremen, and he seems to have carried a long stick which he doubtless used on slackers. In the inscriptions we sometimes see workers receiving strokes with a rod on the usual spot.

That there is more definite evidence of flagellation amongst the ancient Persians we do not find surprising. The horse was adopted in the East from the northern barbarians (to whom the Persians were nearest in this region) long before the Persians are plainly seen in the light of history. While some of the Greeks idealized the Medes and Persians, and the later Hebrew writers could say no ill of their Persian deliverers, it is well known that cruelty in punishment was carried to extreme lengths in Persia, even after the people had become civilized. We are therefore not surprised at stories that the nobles themselves were sometimes severely flagellated. The practice continued from age to age so that even in the Persian stories in *The Arabian Nights* we find offenders visited with the lash.

From the Persians (or possibly the Hittites of Asia Minor) the lash passed to the Syrians, and here, in later Syria, we first find it used in that sort of ascetic self-torment which so frequently gets entangled with sex. As I have described elsewhere, the whole of this region from the Black Sea to the borders of Babylonia and Egypt, and in the earlier time in those kingdoms, was dominated until the first millennium B.C. by a joyous cult of "the Great Mother," the goddess of love and fertility, the divinization of primitive man's Mother Earth. She was honored, even in Judea during several centuries, by sacred prostitution, male and female, in the temples themselves. The cult was in time blended with that of a divine son, a young man god, the annual dying and resurrecting spirit of the sun and vegetation. Whether it was by some weird development (just as in Egypt) of this death of the Great Mother's son or was due to the pressure of the new anti-sex ideas from Persia, a day of mourning came into the chief annual services to the goddess, and here special priests castrated themselves, dug their knives into their limbs, and, as Apuleius describes in his famous story *The Golden Ass,* carried scourges or whips of twisted woollen cords with small (or knuckle) bones fastened in the end of them, with which they flagellated themselves and each other mercilessly on the great festival.

This is the first real instance we have of flagellation on a large scale —for the cult spread from the Syrian desert to Rome—and it is significant that it is intimately connected with sex. We can easily believe that, as Apuleius says, the chief motive of these emasculated priests was to win the applause of the crowds. The theory was that they did honor to their goddess by sharing the sufferings of her son, and there is evi-

7

dence that there were zealots of the cult who paid the same profound respect to the priests as Catholics pay to genuinely ascetic monks. There is also plenty of evidence, even in Rome, that the men earned money by perverse practices. However, we are not here concerned with morals as such. It is enough that we have that association of flagellation and sex which will give us some remarkable pictures of life in the Middle Ages, and presently we shall find also moralists borrowing the lash as an instrument for preserving virtue and some fairly clear indications of men adopting it as an instrument of vice.

It need hardly be said that the Assyrians, being keen horsemen and charioteers, were familiar with the lash and used it on captives and slaves. More interesting is the way in which it passed from the surrounding peoples to the Jews. The early Jewish law, in *Leviticus* and *Deuteronomy,* prescribes scourging for some offenses, but it limits the number of strokes to 40, and the commentations laid down the rule that, to escape the possibility of a transgression of the sacred law by a mistake in counting, the number of strokes should be 39. The author of Acts (V, 40) says that the heads of the Jews in Jerusalem had the apostles of Jesus flogged, and there are several other references to flogging in the New Testament. Jesus is said to have driven the money-changers from the Temple with a whip and is described as receiving the lash himself before he was executed. All this, however, just reflects the well-known use of the lash in the Roman world, and it is of more interest to inquire if the Jews came to use it for self-scourging in the interest of virtue. Theologians read this into Paul's occasional statements that he "chastizes" his body but doubtless that is only a general profession of ascetic practices. Theologians are not agreed.

The Talmud seems to show that the early medieval Jews flogged each other in pairs on the Day of Penitence, and there is evidence that they did so in the later Middle Ages. A theologian of the early part of the 17th Century, Buxtorp, tells us of a quaint custom they then had. At that time there was a custom for two Jews to retire to a corner of the synagogue, where one would lie down and the other would belabor him with a heavy whip. He counted the correct strokes by slowly repeating three times a verse consisting of 13 words. Then he rose and, doubtless after an interval for a little massage, took the whip while the other Jew prostrated himself to receive it. It is clear that this was meant for atonement, not as a moral prophylactic.

The Greek race as a whole had too sane a mind and too healthy a sentiment—one might almost say that they were too artistic—to use the whip much. There is a dubious story that the market police at Athens had whips, and slaves were occasionally flogged, but although the Greeks were horsemen—they had cavalry in the army—we hear little about the whip in most of the Greek countries. Slavery was never extensive amongst the Greeks, and the treatment of slaves was humane in comparison with that of the Romans. In the later or Greek-Roman days we have some evidence of an ascetic use of the whip but we will consider that later.

The Kingdom of Sparta, in the south, was in this, as in most other matters, different from the other Greek kingdoms or republics. We still use the word Spartan in the sense of hard characters and the roughly simple habits of the soldier, and most people will know that the circumstances, like those of the early Roman people, fostered this rigorous training and discipline of the people for military purposes, just as the sheltered position of the Athenians near the coast—and nearest in communication with the easy ways and culture of the cities of Asia Minor —explains their different character. It is time that we abandoned all the old nonsense about the hard, materialistic character of the Spartan and the Roman and the softer or spiritual character of the Athenians.

One of the Spartan institutions which most excited the surprise and disgust of the other Greeks was a Day of Flagellation in connection with the cult of Artemis, the Greek Juno or the ancient mother-earth goddess in a more or less civilized form. The practice seems to have been a blend of the general Spartan custom of going to extremes in the hardening of youth and, possibly, an ancient rite of propitiating the fertility goddess with blood. Before the altar of the goddess youths were flogged to the limit of their power of endurance. Some, in fact, died under the lash and it is said that altars or statues were raised to these in their native places. Apart from the sacred character of the ceremony—priests were present, and a priestess held up a small statue of Artemis in the sight of the boys—it was an occasion of human rivalry between the boys and their families. The mothers, who were present, shrieked at their sons to persevere while the blood streamed from their backs, and it is said—Plutarch himself saw the disgusting ceremony— that the boys eagerly presented themselves for the ordeal. The priests drew omens from the wounds that were inflicted, and crowds gathered for the spectacle. That there would be a sadistic element in the performance we need not doubt, but here flagellation was neither a punishment of crime nor a coercion of the sex impulse. It was part of that hardening of character which was a marked characteristic of the life of the military-minded Spartans. Herodotus, however, tells us that in one part of the kingdom the women themselves were flogged in the temple of Dionysos. On the whole the Greek name for sound sense and feeling is sustained by the poor record of flagellation in the country.

CHAPTER II. THE ROMAN TAKES TO THE WHIP

Every writer on flagellation deals at some length with the brutal use of the whip by the Romans and points out the contrast of the finer character of the Greeks. Most of them forget that the Spartans were as Greek as the Athenians, and the vituperation of the Romans, which suited the purposes of religious apologists, is so obstinate in our literature that more emphasis than ever was laid on it at a time when, in the 18th and early 19th Century, the lash was used in Christendom, from the slave-states of America to the penal colonies of Australia, as brutally as it had ever been in ancient Rome. Moreover, in some there was a strong public sentiment against using it on the bodies of free men, and the whipping of slaves was restricted in the 2nd Century A.D. by the Stoic Emperors and, like other old brutalities, was far less in the last century of the Empire than it was even 100 years ago. In fact, these "hard" and "brutal" Romans established from the 2nd Century onward the greatest system of charity or philanthropy that the world ever saw until modern times.

I have elsewhere described this evolution of Roman character, and in the preceding chapter I said a few words about the way in which modern psychology and history have discredited this kind of rhetoric about the "genius" or hereditary spirit or character of peoples. On these lines we understand that hardness of the early Roman character which persisted in later ages in such things as the use of the lash and the games of the amphitheater. It is a matter of geographical accident that the ancestors of the Greeks, who had belonged to a common family with those of the Romans, settled more to the east of the Danube region and, when the migration south began, crossed the mountains into Greece, where they were nearest to the area of civilization, while the Romans were farthest from it and out of touch with it until they came to build ships. It is again a matter of geography that the Athenians settled in a sheltered area while the Romans had to cut their way through a number of settled peoples and to maintain their position age after age by force of arms. It is a matter of geography that the mountains, largely of barren character, of Greece caused an early and extensive migration overseas and contact with civilization while the Romans had no such drive. There are a dozen contrasts in their environment but it is enough here to say that it impressed an aggressive military character on the Romans as surely as the northern conditions gave the Teutons and Scandinavians their pale skin, blue eyes, and blond hair; and that the aggressive wars that ensued gave the Romans enormous masses of slave captives whom they inevitably ruled by the whip.

In the early centuries of Roman history the law did not cross the threshold of a man's house and he had power of life and death over his slaves. He had the same power over his wife and daughters, and doubtless they also tasted the lash, but there is evidence that the father did not, as a rule, use his authority harshly except in dealing with the slaves. In the two centuries immediately preceding the Christian Era the number of slave captives became enormous, and once or twice they organized and made bloody revolts. The lash fell all the more brutally upon them, and there is no need to enlarge on that age of flagellation. The leather thongs or twisted cords were made more cruel by fastening knuckle bones and even lead or iron or wire in the ends, and many a slave died under the lash. Often a weight was fastened to their legs as they were suspended from a beam so that they could not kick the flogger.

In the 1st Century of the Christian Era there were two notable developments. We have so persistent a literary tradition of libeling the

Romans that only the first of these is mentioned by most writers. It is that the Roman ladies, who had now won a considerable independence of their husbands, including the right to hold great wealth and therefore large bodies (sometimes hundreds) of domestic slaves, to a serious extent degenerated in character and had their slaves flogged, often for trivial offenses, with all the old brutality.

We have to keep in mind that most of these stories of the brutality and looseness of patrician ladies in that century came from the satirical poet *Juvenal,* a fierce opponent of the rich and entirely unscrupulous about the truth of his statements, many of which are easily shown to be false. But other writers confirm that many of the ladies were ruthless in the treatment of the slaves. The men who spilt a little wine or soup at dinner, the maid who slipped in attending to the mistress's toilet, would, often in the lady's presence, be brutally flogged. It is said that some mistresses made the girls wait on them in the bedroom stripped to the waist as a reminder that the least fault would bring the lash, and that some mistresses wielded it themselves. That there was a good deal of sadism in all this we cannot doubt, but the scanty evidence does not permit us to do more than speculate on that aspect. Sometimes a lady would have slaves brutally flogged (it is said) to entertain her friends at a banquet, and in such cases the sex element is apparent. In other cases the masters would have male intruders, often of their own rank, severely flogged. These amorous adventures used to dress as female slaves to get into a mansion to see the mistress or daughter, and if they were caught the master affected to regard them as slaves. It is said that the historian Sallust once paid the price of this sort of gallantry. It is also said of the Emperor Caligula that if any man distracted him in the theater he had him stripped and flogged him with his own hand.

A lighter type of whip was used habitually in the schools. The Roman schoolmaster—there were schools for all the children—believed strongly in the maxim, "Spare the whip and spoil the child," or, as the ancient Egyptian masters put it, "A boy's ears grow on his back." Even the Vestal Virgins, the select sacred virgins of the Roman community, were flogged for offenses that were not serious enough to incur the death penalty. They were, however, covered with a veil when the priest used the whip on them. Statues of the gods, even of Venus, had a whip in their hand, and whips of three different types were hung up in courts of justice. Delinquent soldiers were heavily beaten, but this seems to have been with the rods which, tied in a bundle with an axe, were carried by lower officers on the march.

But a new development, which only experts describe because it conflicts with what religious writers say about the Romans, began in the 1st Century. The master's absolute power over his slaves was in fact nullified by law long before the beginning of the Christian Era, and to kill a slave was largely classed as murder. In the 1st Century imperial decrees, the Roman equivalent of laws, gave the slave the right to prosecute a master for cruelty, and we must conclude that the more savage kind of flogging was checked. The moralist Seneca, who had considerable influence on Nero in his earlier years, repeatedly says in his essays, following Epicurus, that the slave is "a friend of lower degree," and he sternly denounced cruelty to slaves. The Emperor Hadrian, also an Epicurean, sent into exile a rich and noble Roman lady for defying the law and treating her slaves with cruelty. In the last two centuries of the pagan Empire we meet little evidence of the old brutal type of flagellation, and the martyr stories which represent the Roman authorities cruelly beating the Christians are now acknowledged even by Catholic experts to be forgeries in nine cases out of 10.

More interesting is the fact that the bishops, when they won power over the emperors and therefore over the laws in the first half of the 4th Century, did not interfere with a kind of flagellation on the public streets which was not only what they would call an obscene exhibition but was explicitly motivated by a mixture of paganism and sex which ought to have seemed to them outrageous. This was the festival of the

Lupercalia. The Lupercal was a cave shrine of great antiquity and prestige under the shelter of the Palatine Hill (on which the imperial palace was), and when the sacrifices were performed here on February 15 a number of men daubed with blood of the victims who wore no clothes but carried a strip or whip of goatskin, ran through the city slapping, either on the palm of the hand or on the belly, the women they met. It was, of course, in theory a fertility rite, and the women offered their bodies freely. In the later period of the empire the woman stripped themselves, and the whole thing must have taken on rather the nature of an orgy. That it had once been seriously regarded is clear from the fact that only young men of the highest families, who vied with each other for the honor (or pleasure), were enrolled in the rank of these Lupercal priests. Mark Antony, Caesar's rival, once served in the festival.

The bishops had first induced the emperors to pass penal laws against the practice of paganism in 357, and laws of increasing severity were passed up to 400, when paganism was considered to have been forcibly suppressed. Yet this indecent and essentially pagan festival continued in the city of Rome until the year 476, the people vigorously refusing to abandon it. By this late date Goths and Vandals had more than decimated the population and left the city in a miserable condition, so Pope Gelasius, a vigorous and strongly religious man, attacked the ceremony. He was himself vigorously assailed by his people and had to publish an Apology, but such civil power as there was then in Rome was controlled by the Pope, and the picturesque ceremony had to be abandoned. It is chiefly from the Pope's own letter that we learn that the women had by this time begun to strip themselves. He speaks of the "nations who receive blows on their naked bodies."

Meantime another kind of flagellation had, in the 4th Century, spread under Christian influence. Flogging was one of the penalties imposed upon pagans and heretics by imperial law, and it was therefore natural that, when the great controversy about the divinity of Christ rent the Church into two fairly equal halves, each side should begin flogging the other side as heretics. I have amply shown elsewhere, from the writings and sermons of the contemporary Fathers, that the Romans and Greeks of the 4th Century had not changed their morals in crossing the street from the temple to the church, and sex had its place in the world disorders that occurred during a quarter of a century. Both sides, the Unitarians (Arians) and Trinitarians, now had bodies of young women who professed to be sacred virgins—St. Jerome has a scalding description of their morals—and it was especially these who were flogged. They were stripped naked by their opponents and commonly thrashed on their buttocks with branches of thorn bushes, and then they were sometimes made to sit, still naked, on hot iron plates.

The strange mixture of virtue and vice in connection with flagellation was thus clear enough in the 4th Century, but it is of more interest to inquire whether in the Greek-Roman or pagan world itself we have evidence of a use of the lash, self-administered, either for the restriction or the excitement of the sex impulse. There is plenty of evidence for ascetic self-scourging. It is now commonly acknowledged by writers of any real knowledge that there was a considerable development of moral ideas in the few centuries before Christ. This is reflected in the Old Testament, when the books are read in their proper chronological order, but the Jews learned it from their neighbors, especially the Persians and the Greeks. The Greek moralists generally held to the social theory of the code of conduct and rarely felt into ethical mysticism, but the Persian sacred books strongly reprobated "the flesh" and taught that there was a hell for sexual sinners. This doctrine had a strange appeal to a certain number of individuals in all parts of the Greek-Roman world besides being incorporated in certain ascetic Jewish sects, in Christianity, and in Manicheanism, its great rival in the 4th Century.

That many of the Roman and Greek moralists (Epictetus, Plutarch,

12

Apollonius, etc.) urged an ascetic manner of life in the interest of virtue is well known, and some of these went so far as to recommend self-flagellation. Lucian says in his Dialogues that in his own day—2nd Century—there were philosophers who advised young men to use the whip on themselves if they would preserve their virtue. Philostratus says in his *Life of Appolonius of Tyana* that Greeks who adhered to the cult of the Scythian Diana were told by the oracles that they must scourge themselves before the altar. There was, Lucian says, a Cynic of Trojan's days who, complaining of temptation, used to scourge himself or get others to whip him on his buttocks, before a crowd of people. It is piquant that this habit of self-scourging which has always been thought distinctly Christian, was urged by a number of pagan moralists and seems to have been fairly extensively practiced amongst the followers of the more mystic moralists and the stricter religions. But we must remember that while the pre-Christian moralists condemned adultery, as an invasion of the right of others, they rarely condemned simple fornication—even Zeno, the founder of the Stoics, was liberal in this respect—and thought prostitution a natural and legitimate social institution.

To the modern mind it is a more interesting question whether this Greek-Roman age, which in so many respects resembled the modern age, affords any evidence of that perverse use of the lash which sexologists show to be fairly common in modern times. Religious folk, who talk eloquently about the vices and "swinish lusts" of the pagan world, about which they would think it a sin to read, would be astonished to learn, if one could teach them anything on such matters, that there is more evidence of this sort of morbidity in the Middle Ages and much more in modern times than in the Greek-Roman world. A distinguished German physician of the 17th Century who seems to have been at the same time a remarkable classical scholar, Q. H. Meibom, has left us a little Latin work (*De flagrorum usu in re venerea,* 1670) on the subject. He, it seems, discussed it with a group of medical friends and, finding them unwilling to believe that such a thing was ever done, made a diligent search both of the classics and medieval literature. He finds only one short allusion to it in Latin literature but many instances in his own age.

I will give the medieval cases later. The Latin reference is taken from Petronius, one of the freer writers of the 1st Century, a sybarite and a courtier of the Emperor Nero. It is a short and incidental statement that a Roman who was afflicted with impotence went to the temple of Priapus for advice. I may not give a literal translation of the advice of the "priest of Priapus" and must be content to say that the recipe included "gently beating his body from the navel downward with a bunch of green nettles." In a writer like Petronius this is probably a bit of Roman gossip but we are justified in concluding that the idea or the practice was known in Rome. Meibom shows that ancient medical writers recommended it as a cure of melancholia or other mental disorders in connection with sex, anemia, and constipation. The general idea was, I think, that it brought about its effect by inducing heat.

Apart from this there is a passage in that most outspoken of saints, Jerome, which Meibom does not give because on the face of it there is no sexual implication. Jerome says that "in Rome there were men who were filthy enough to expose their buttocks in the public markets or the open streets and to suffer themselves to be lashed by a pretended conjuror." So the learned theologian Boileau translates him; and some early Christian writers tell us that what the Romans called "flagratores were men who allowed themselves to be whipped or who whipped others for money." Putting the two together it is clear that there were street corner entertainers in Rome who either offered their own persons to be whipped and then sent the hat around the crowd or offered small sums to thick-skinned members of the crowd to provide a spectacle and then took the usual collection. There were incidents of street life in the coarser quarters of English towns in my own boyhood which were not far removed from this. There were worse scenes in the streets in the Middle Ages, and no one with a good knowledge of the Roman workers will question that these things were possible. Some of these refined critics say that St. Jerome could not possibly have written "buttocks," which is *nates* in Latin, but must have said *nares*, which means nostrils. It would hardly move Jerome to call it "filthy" if it were merely a tap on the nose. In his letters he especially uses the coarsest language himself, even to young ladies. The shows would hardly have been tolerated by the police in the Forum, as Jerome suggests, but seem to have been common in the narrow, crowded cross-streets of the Subura or the Velabrum. That there was a strong spice of sex in such exhibitions is so obvious that I need not discuss it.

These first explicit references to what the medieval theologians called "the lower discipline" lead one of the early clerical writers on the subject to give us an elegant and singular dissertation on that indelicate organ. The most frequently quoted writer on flagellation, "the Rev. W. Cooper"—I will explain presently that he was not a cleric—pretends to quote this little essay from the Latin work on flagellation of the learned canon of Paris and doctor of the Sorbonne, Boileau. In point of fact it is an English translator (and enlarger) of Boileau's book who wrote it, and, though this man remains anonymous, I gather from a French copy of his original work or an inscription on the fly-leaf that it is the work of a French priest, the Abbé Granet. In the gay medieval style, which still lingered in the 18th Century, the priest begins his eulogy:

> The part we mention is that part on which a man sits and is of itself exceedingly deserving of our esteem. It is in the first place a characteristic part and appendage of mankind. It is formed by the expansion of muscles that exist in no other animal and are entirely proper to the human species . . . by allowing him to sit it enables him to calculate the motions, whether real or apparent, of the stars, to ascertain their revolutions and foreknow their periodical returns. It puts him in a condition to promote the liberal Arts and Sciences, Music, Painting, Algebra, Geometry, and the rest, not to mention the whole tribe of mechanical arts and manufactures! . . . It is said to be as important as the head in studying law, for it is a saying in the universities that in order to succeed in that study a man must have an iron head and a leaden arse."

But when the reverend gentleman goes on to discuss the matter from the artistic angle and quotes Roman and French poets, which he does through several pages, I must refrain from reproducing his words or those of the poets. We no longer live in an age of such freedom. We do not go to church.

CHAPTER III. THE EARLY CHRISTIANS AND THE SCOURGE

To the modern reader the word flagellation suggests not so much the whipping of criminals, slaves, schoolboys, or sailors, which he assumes to have been practiced in all ages, as the self-scourging of the ascetic, in which the sex element is subtly implicated, and the morbid use of the whip that engages the attention of our sexologists. On a superficial knowledge we are tempted to say that the first, the flagellation of offenders, is mainly a feature of pagan days, self-flagellation in the interest of virtue a feature of the ages of faith, and the third variety a novelty of modern times.

We have already seen that this view is false. Scourging was as brutal during the long Middle Ages and, in early modern times, on the American cotton plantations or in the British navy, colonies, and the jails, as it had been in ancient Rome. We saw further that ascetic self-scourging was not introduced by Christian moralists, and in fact, there seems to have been a reluctance of the earliest Chrisian ascetics to indulge in that particular form of self-torture. Whether this was because the wiser of them had noticed that by some strange freak the instrument which was used to drive out the devil seemed to let in the devil, or because, as some apologists say, the whip was too closely identified with delinquent slaves or was put to such base uses as St. Jerome describes, is a matter of speculation. But it is historically correct that during the first four centuries of the Christian Era it is rare to find a religious leader recommending self-flagellation for the mortification of the flesh.

Apart from those morbid practices which particularly interest the sexologist our scanty literature on this subject is mainly based upon a few Christian writers of the 17th and 18th centuries. I have already quoted the first of these, Meibom, to whom we are indebted for a search of the classics and a special study of what he calls, in the title of his book, the relation of flagellation to "venereal things." The second was Jacques Boileau, whose Latin work, *Historia Flagellantium* (History of Flagellants, with the sub-title "On the proper and improper use of the scourge amongst Christians," 1700), is much quoted by all subsequent writers and learnedly covers the entire Christian period to about the end of the 17th Century.

This Boileau, it is interesting to note, was a learned canon of the Royal Chapel at Paris and doctor of theology of the Sorbonne. But the air of piety that one notices in his work is largely forced. His brother, one of the great French poets, Boileau-Despréaux, said of him that if he had not been a doctor of the Sorbonne (the theological university) he would have made a good doctor of Italian Comedy. Although, as I said, Cooper wrongly attributes to him the eulogy of the human seat which I quoted, he is extremely free in some of his works, and it is said that he told a friend that he wrote in Latin so that the bishops would not be able to read him. His other works are tinged with anti-clerical satire of an amiable nature, and the Jesuits savagely attacked him. His brother, the famous poet, was an acknowledged Freethinker.

I do not know whether there is any copy in America of an old English translation of this work, with extensive and learned additions, which was published anonymously in London in 1784 with the title *Memorials of Human Superstition*. The copy in the British Museum has a note on the fly-leaf, apparently by one who bought the work at the time, saying that the author was the Abbé Granet, probably one of the many French refugees in England, though in those days an abbé was not necessarily a priest. I recommend this to the reader who can get access to a copy in preference to Boileau's work with its forced air of piety and virtue. The style is elegant and free, and the additions are valuable.

As far as the early Christian centuries are concerned Boileau's work is, as the translator points out, not quite reliable. He had a Rabelais-ean scorn of the monastic asceticism of the Middle Ages which (including self-flagellation) the Jesuits were trying to restore in his time. He therefore wanted to prove that the early Fathers, even in the Egyptian desert, did not approve of the use of the whip: that in fact there was comparatively little use of it until Cardinal Peter Damiani, the fanatical leader of the monastic movement of the 11th Century, imposed it upon the Church. To this argument Boileau's clerical opponents shrieked that his work was "an insult to the saints, of both sexes, who practiced the lower discipline," as if these and the early Fathers had considered it improper. "Discipline," which is still the word for self-flagellation in the Catholic world, is an abbreviation of "the discipline of the scourge," and there was in the later Middle Ages a resounding controversy as to whether the "lower discipline" (on the buttocks and thighs) was just as proper and legitimate as the "upper discipline" (on the back).

It may be useful to warn the reader, incidentally, that the zeal of modern Catholic writers to prove that in the Middle Ages the discipline was not taken or given naked, especially in the case of women, is due to the falsification of the character and tastes of the Middle Ages in their own literature. I remember a heated controversy in the last century when a distinguished painter exhibited a picture of a female saint —St. Elizabeth of Hungary, I think—taking her vows bending nude before an altar while her friar confessor (not with closed eyes) stood by. The priests bitterly attacked the painter, whom Huxley defended, claiming that in medieval Latin "nude" commonly meant clad only in underwear or semi-nude. It does sometimes mean that the inner tunic or shift, which the rich wore, was retained, but the critics seemed to have an idea that even in those days folk wore washable underlinen and were as coy as they are today about appearing without it. We shall see that that is nonsense. There was no such feeling about exposure in the Middle Ages. Obscene carvings have had to be removed in modern times from the facades of French cathedrals. Irish churches commonly had, in some cases until the last century, a Sheil-na-gig or figure of a nude woman crouching with grossly realistic sex parts over the door of the church to keep out evil spirits; and doubtless the Irish maids and youths then went in and prayed for help against temptation. Companies of naked prostitutes walked in civic processions. The servants of a manor or pilgrims at an inn, of both sexes, undressed and slept in one large room, and even their betters often slept seven or eight in a bed. In Papal Rome certain offenders were compelled to march through the public streets in broad daylight with their single tunics raised above the waist precisely to prove their sex.

But Boileau, whom I suspect to have been particularly concerned about the lower discipline because the subject lent itself to disguised frivolity, goes farther and does not fairly present the evidence of flagellation in earlier Christian times so that he can more easily blame the later period. He seems to be right when he says that the Church Fathers did not recommend flagellation. Even Jerome, who was ascetic (except in language), does not speak of practicing it, and never recommends it in his letters. Even what are called the Fathers of the Desert, the leaders of the Christians who took refuge in the Egyptian desert from the pagan persecutors and became legions of monks and hermits, are not described as including flagellation amongst their weird practices. They lived at the top of pillars (which must have stunk like a hyena's den) for years, deliberately cultivated lice on their persons, and preserved their virtue by all sorts of picturesque horrors, but we read little of scourging before the 5th Century, when some of the early monastic rules begin to enjoin it. By this time it was generally recognized as a cure for heresy and Christians flogged their slaves—sometimes to death.

as Church councils tell us—as merrily as ever, but it does not seem yet to have been popular as a guardian of virtue. According to the Fathers (Jerome, Augustine, Chrysostom, Salvianus, etc.), in fact, very few, even of the crowds of monks, were interested in methods of restraining their lusts. They felt that it was easier and more agreeable to let them loose.

It is of little interest to give every reference to flagellation that we find at this period. For the 4th and 5th centuries hardly more than half a dozen cases are quoted but some of them seem to point to a wide practice. Boileau himself gives two monastic leaders of the 4th Century who praised the scourge, and St. Augustine says that a few of the bishops of his time included it among the penalties they imposed. St. Basil of Caesarea speaks of churches in which three scourges hung: one for delinquent monks, one for thieves, and one for the local laity. In some legends of hermits of the time it is said that the devils thrashed the saints, so many might legitimately distrust the lash. In all these cases, however, it is a question of punishing defenders, and we may take it that Roman practices so far survived that the lash was freely used for that purpose. The Teutonic tribes that had invaded the Roman world had now settled in kingdoms, and in western Europe they included severe scourging in their penal codes. Roman civilization was dead, and Europe was becoming steadily more boorish and brutal.

About the 7th Century the practice of self-flagellation spread in the monasteries. Hitherto the men who professed to the monks were a vast army of what we might call amateurs, in large part without settled abode, discipline, or authority. The meaning of the "founding" of orders by men like St. Benedict, who himself scathingly describes the vast masses of vagabond and disorderly "monks" of his time, is that they drew up a strict rule of life and acknowledged as followers only those who lived in large regular communities under abbots. Some of these founders insisted on self-flagellation, though there was soon a difference of opinion as to whether or no they should be stripped. The learned ecclesiastical historian Du Cange quotes the following from the unpublished manuscript of an early monastic code:

> The monk must rise from his knees, modestly take off his clothes, then lie down again naked to his middle. When the whipping is over they must help him to put on his clothes.

This, of course, refers to the whipping of a delinquent monk—he may merely have broken a jug or spilled the soup—in what was called the "chapter" or periodical assembly of all the inmates of a monastery for confession of faults and exhortation to virtue. Church councils and the laws of some countries had decided that a scourging, which had so long been the punishment of a slave, no longer put a mark of infamy on a man, and it spread more easily. Pope Gregory the Great warmly encouraged it in the monasteries, and we may suppose that it was general in regular monasteries by the end of the 7th Century. What proportion of the monasteries that now appeared in their thousands in Europe *were* strict is a question I have examined elsewhere. Briefly, during most ages of medieval history the great majority of the monasteries, of both sexes (and often monks and nuns were in one building), were corrupt, so that we must not imagine that a large part of the population was now addicted to self-torture.

We may, in fact, assume that the men and women who in so sordid and licentious an age as it was seriously devoted themselves to self-flagellation seemed to the mass of the people heroes of virtue and entered the local chronicles as saints. Although these chronicles, especially of the first half of the Middle Ages (the Dark Age), are full of the most preposterous rubbish, and it would be quite arbitrary to laugh at all the miracles and accept implicitly all the stories of holy actions, the ecclesiastical writers who are familiar with the chronicles give us comparatively few cases of self-flagellation. The kind of self-scourging which was a matter of routine in the regular monasteries was doubtless as innocent as the "discipline" which we monks of modern times—I was, as most of my readers probably know, a monk from the age of 16 to 28—used to have to inflict upon ourselves twice a week. I may describe it better and will say only that in all ages, even the most depraved, there was always a few men and women who carried out their creed to its logical extreme. Amongst these self-flagellation became a common practice from the 7th Century onward.

While Europe sank deeper and deeper, until the 11th Century, in the scale of morals and culture, these mortifiers of the flesh vied with each other in the ferocity of their assaults upon themselves. There was one who locked himself in his monastic cell with a lash in each hand and, while he recited penitential psalms, thrashed himself with all his strength. He estimated that it took 3,000 strokes of the whip to atone for a single year's growth of peccadilloes. The champion of the class, whose fame went all over Europe and down the ages, was a St. Dominic Loricati, who stripped himself naked and went to work with a hefty whip in each hand. He included his scourges in his baggage when he traveled as one now does a tooth brush. And the pious monastic chroniclers assure us that all these men lived to a ripe old age. One died prematurely at the age of 84, one at 120, and one at 140. It does not seem to have occurred to them that it was hard for such good men to to be kept so long out of heaven. But I have already given the warning that the chronicles of these centuries are as a rule compilations of the gossip of a grossly ignorant and credulous age. Apart from the priests —and they were to a great extent barely able to read—it is probable that not more than one in 100 could read and write.

Although at that time it was usual for a man or woman who "got religion" to quit wife or husband and go off to a monastery there was a minority of pious lay folk, and the practice of self-flagellation spread to them. There is some evidence that priests now began to compel female penitents to submit to be flogged by them, but a yearly confession to a priest was not obligatory until some centuries later and we may postpone the consideration of that aspect of the disease. It is usually royal or noble self-torturers, partly because they were so rare—and just as rare in the category at this time are the names of bishops and archbishops—whose piety is entered in the chronicles. In England in the 10th Century there was a truculent monk of the type that loved flogging, St. Dunstan. King Edgar took a pretty nun from her convent, which seems to have been a not infrequent occurrence, and Dunstan, who intimidated the young king, was content with an expression of repentance and a few more concessions to the clergy. But when a noble of his court did the same, and was even protected by the king, Dunstan demanded the lash. The noble had to come before a general council of the higher clergy in his bare feet and a coarse woollen tunic, carrying a scourge in his hand. He had to kneel at the feet of Dunstan and receive the lash.

In the previous year, 969, an incident had occurred at the other extreme of civilization, Constantinople, which shows how the use of the lash was now again universal. A tax-gatherer of the Emperor Nicephorus ventured to demand tribute from the monks of a large monastery. When the monks pleaded dire poverty—probably after hiding their treasure—and inability to pay anything he put their leaders in chains and threatened further punishment. The monks in their poverty and helplessness prayed to their patron St. Nikon and, the story runs, the saint came down from heaven that night and gave the man a sound whipping. It is not difficult to guess who really wielded the lash, but the story, as usual, circulated throughout Christendom and is solemnly included in the enormous Church History of Cardinal Baronius, the Father of Catholic History.

Of authentic stories before the 11th Century we have few and they are of little interest. Europe was almost incredibly debased, and its literature is for the most part gross and unreliable. Only in Italy, where

18

the Lombards had rekindled a little civilization could men write decent Latin, and, though they were clerics, the writers were not of the ascetic school. The Papacy itself remained for more than a century at its lowest depth of depravity, perjurers, rapers, sodomists, adulterers, and even murderers almost succeeding each other on the Papal throne from 905 to 1040. Civilization was almost confined to the Moslem or Arab southern half of Spain, which was far removed from any disposition to lay the lash on its own shoulders and was in fact remarkably free from violence. But from Spain, through Marseilles and the South of France, a higher standard of taste was slowly breaking upon Europe, and the heavier and more boorish violence was being modified. With this, for a time, the use of the lash was neglected. One of the nobles who stands out in the chronicles of the 10th Century as a lay-monk who used to flagellate himself severely was William, Duke of Aquitain. His descendant in the latter half of the 11th Century was, from the church angle, a devil. He was the first of the troubadours whose songs have come down to us and has good title to be called the most frivolous, most licentious, and most civilized prince in Christendom. His daughter Eleanor enlivened two courts with her gaiety in successive marriages and was one of the leaders in the new Courts of Love.

On the whole we may say that the first thousand years of Christian history were not much disfigured with blood that was shed by a man's own hand (or whip). From the words of Church councils and codes of law which I have quoted it seems that, on account of the long association of the whip with the slave, a flogging impressed upon a free man some such stigma of infamy as a sojourn in Sing Sing does today. This may have something to do with the reluctance of most of the early ascetics to use the lash. Church and state removed the infamy, and the monastic bodies began to include the lash amongst their penances. Where we have positive knowledge of the life of these monastic bodies, as in the letters of St. Boniface on the monasteries of Germany, France and England, we find such general license that we need waste no sympathy. There must have been 1,000 kisses to one stripe. Reformers of monasteries rose age after age but in a few decades, sometimes years, the license in the few reformed houses was as bad as ever. Here and there were really decent abbots who read such literature as was available and took their Christian creed soberly without ascetic excess. Considering the enormous number of monasteries for so small and miserably poor a population as Europe then had these good and sensible abbots were rare. You can hardly gather the names of a dozen in a century. But a few reforms of monasteries in France, which spread to Germany, happened to coincide with the introduction of some sort of civilization into Saxony through a prince marrying a Greek princess, and this led to the strangest development of the practice of flagellation.

CHAPTER IV. THE GOLDEN AGE OF PIOUS FLAGELLATION

The few works on this subject that we have generally exasperate the reader by their lack of chronological order and complete failure to explain why the different developments in connection with flagellation took place. All say that an Italian monk, Cardinal Peter Damiani, brought about a remarkable fervor for self-scourging in the 11th Century and this prepared the way for the extraordinary outbreak of the Flagellants of the 13th and 14th centuries. But the reader who knows the kind of historical manual which says that the barbaric invasions now ended and the Church was able to exert its fragrant influence is is puzzled. For just at the time when the reformed monks captured the Papacy and several princes and kindled a sort of religious revival in the Church, Europe entered upon a new period of license which in the matter of sexual freedom matches, if it does not surpass, any period in ancient Greece and Rome: the age of what is called Chivalry and the Troubadours, in which we really find the most aggressive and unrestrained body of women in history and a literature which, in large part, no one would dare to translate and publish today.

At this interesting stage of European history, the second part of the 11th Century, in short, we have a curious collection of simultaneous developments. All authorities admit that Europe, mainly through contact with the Arabs, began to recover civilization or advance fairly rapidly in art, culture, amenity of life, education, and social organization. The root of this was, of course, a rise of economic level (industry, trade, and the circulation of money), which had been unimaginably low for the five or six centuries of the Dark Age. This automatically led to concentrations of wealth in cities and abbeys and the religious art (in form) which is sophistically represented as proof that Europe had become more religious. Further proof is said to be found in the Crusades, whereas every competent historian recognizes that these were expeditions in search of loot and fighting and were just (like the bloody tournaments) an expression of the savagery of the Knights; and in the rise of new bodies of monks, whereas it is obvious that these mean that the older orders of monks were so corrupt that a really religious man or woman could not join them. Here I must not even sum up the analysis of the age I have given in larger works. Briefly, there was no rise whatever of the general moral level of Europe, not only in regard to what the Church called sins of the flesh but in regard to violence, torture, injustice and dishonor. You might call the first part of the Middle Ages, the Dark Age (roughly 450 to 1050), Savagery in Homespun and the second part (1050 to 1550 or longer) Savagery in Silk.

Thus this spread of a zeal for self-flagellation which occurred in the second half of the 11th Century coincides with a general advance of civilization in respect of art, culture, and civic organization and at the same time with an extraordinary growth of sexual freedom in the richer class (princes, nobles, knights, and ladies). The solution of the paradox is that the new ascetic movement was not nearly so widespread as writers on the subject imagine. It was one of those limited and temporary puritan movements which occur periodically in the history of Christendom. And in the form it took, heavy self-scourging, it reflects the contemporary increasing brutality of law and life.

I said that there were two streams of civilization flowing into the arid desert of Dark Age barbarism. One was the example of the brilliant Arab civilization in Spain and (to a much less degree) in the East. This acted more slowly on account of the deadly prejudice against

20

"pagans," but is was the main source of the advances in real civilization and was at the opposite pole of thought from asceticism. In the 10th Century the Germans had sent a diplomatic mission, headed by a strict and dirty monk, to the Arab-Spanish court. They had treated him with wondering courtesy but had regarded him as they might have done an imported baboon or chimpanzee. The other stream was from Germany and, while it did bear some elements of art and culture, because a German prince had married a Greek princess and her suite had brought some cleaner air into Germany, it was the source of the new asceticism. You might almost say that the Germans learned to take their religion seriously before they were properly civilized and so gave it this barbaric form.

The German court, or court of the Holy Roman Empire, was stimulated in the 10th Century by the monk zealots who were protected at it to make an end of the century-old degradation of the Papacy. Roman corruption beat them, in spite of their formidable armies, every time until Henry II, who is in the calendar as a saint, came to the throne about the year 1000. The chronicles say that Henry was so humble and pious that every time he was going to put on his crown he got his confessor to flagellate him: a sort of apology to Christ for a mere mortal daring to wear a crown. Still the Romans defied them and poisoned off the pious German Popes they set up, and it was an Italian monk, Hildebrand (later Pope Gregory VII), who reached the German court from one of the strict monasteries of France, that after a ferocious and protracted struggle led them to victory. He was a man of terrific energy and clerical ambition, and he gathered about him puritan birds of the same feather—quite unscrupulous in fighting for a pious cause, tough men of peasant extraction (like himself)—and in the garb of humility cultivating the roar of a tyrant. They imposed celibacy (and irregular connections) upon the priests throughout the Church by spurring ignorant mobs to thrash, cudgel, and sack the houses of married priests and their wives and by working upon princes and noble ladies who had more virtue than wit; and by unscrupulous political alliances they got the troops for the enforcement of their ideas of virtue.

While the whole group of these ascetics cooperated in demoralizing the clergy by forbidding them to marry, Hildebrand devoted himself especially to strengthening the power of the Papacy, and his friend and chief lieutenant Peter Damiani to what he called the purification of morals. This was the man whom all writers consider mainly responsible for the growth of flagellation. He had begun life as a swineherd and, though he ended it as a cardinal or "prince of church," he remained to the end of his life as master of the swineherd's vocabulary and kept his fierce energy. Here is a sample of his preaching to the mob during his campaign to suppress clerical marriage. He is speaking of the legal wives of the priests:

> I address myself to you, you darlings of the priests, you tit-bits of the devil, poison of minds, daggers of souls, aconite of drinkers, bane of eaters, stuff of sin, occasion of destruction. To you I turn, I say you gynecaea of the ancient enemy, you hoopoes, vampires, bats, leeches, wolves. Come and hear me, you whores, you wallowing beds for fat swine, you bedrooms of unclean spirits, you nymphs, you sirens, you harpies, you Dianas, you wicked tigresses, you furious vipers . . .

In this language he recommended the virtues of the gentle Virgin to the people of Italy. Then the mob dispersed to strip and assault the wives, rob and thrash the priests, whose marriages had to that time been perfectly legitimate in both civil and ecclesiastical law. Damiani wrote, and presented to the Pope, who warmly approved it, a little work on the vices (particularly sodomy and bestiality) of the bishops, priests, and monks. A modern historian says of it that "nothing in Aristophanes, Athenaeus, or Petronius gives a picture of more bestial depravity than the one drawn by a prince of the Church of the manners of his clerical contemporaries." You may ask if the pious fool thought that he would

21

really cure these vices by taking away the priests' legal and respectable wives. But he relied above all on his favorite argument—the whip.

The savagery in the strict monasteries—fortunately still only a small minority—now went so far that abbots cut out the eyes of their monks for immorality. There is a case approved by the Pope in one of his letters. The self-scourging was fierce. The last reform of the monasteries, a few decades earlier, had spent its fervor in most cases but a new zealot, Bernard of Clairveaux, organized a new reform, the Cistercians, and the stories of their heroic scourgings spread over Europe. As a matter of fact most writers on flagellation have an exaggerated idea of the amount of blood that was shed. These hectic phases never spread far or lasted long. A non-Catholic historical writer says:

> Bernard became a monk of Citeaux in 1113, and the order within little more than a century after its foundation was in possession of more than 1,800 abbeys in France, Germany, England, Ireland, Denmark, Norway, and Sweden.

He seems to imagine them almost swimming with blood. As a matter of fact, within 50 years most of them were rich and jolly houses with great stores of liquor and venison, buffoons, music and song, horses and hounds, and ample compensation for the flesh. When Abelard became a monk after his castration and ordered his wife Heloise to enter a nunnery, she asked him where there was one fit for a decent woman to live in; and later Abelard himself gave a scathing account of the condition of the monasteries generally.

There are, by the way, a few passages in Abelard's letters to Heloise which raise the question whether the stimulating use of the whip was not known at the time. In one place he reminds her that "occasionally I beat you not from anger but from love." Some conclude that Heloise was coy and reluctant and Abelard used violence to make her consent. They cannot have read her letters to him. Even years later, when she was the abbess of a convent, the freedom of her language is extraordinary. But I do not find any other allusion to the use of the lash as a stimulant until some centuries later. Few needed stimulation in that full-blooded age. Havelock Ellis makes the mistake of saying that the knights, burdened with heavy armor and riding all day, were slow. He had misinterpreted the evidence that in those days the *women*, maid or matron, pursued the *men*. All experts acknowledge that it was an age of extraordinary and general female aggressiveness. Yet the knights themselves were as sexy as apes.

What is of more interest than the self-flagellation of the monks in a few strict monasteries is the extent of the custom among the laity. It is, as usual, chiefly noble penitents who enter the chronicles, but as the princes, nobles, and knights generally took no notice of the Christian code of sex behavior, we have not many individual cases. St. Louis, King of France, is one. "I did not know that I was marrying a monk," Queen Eleanor, one of the gay ladies of the time, said when she asked the priests to find some flaw in her marriage to him. They obliged her (and the king) by finding that their great-great grandparents had been related, so the marriage was void, and Eleanor went to promote free love in England. She was a typical great lady of the time. But Louis is in the calendar as a saint. In the Royal (or Holy) Chapel at Paris there is a representation of him in a stained glass window being scourged. One must not imagine his suffering severely. The Chroniclers explain that he was a man of unusually thin skin, so doubtless his confessor laid on with discretion.

The plea of tender skin and danger to health was countered by the puritans with stories about the unhappy end of pious folk who had avoided flagellation on that plea. One was a story of a holy canon who had made this excuse. He appeared after death to a friend and told him that he had had a stormy passage. "There was," he said, "not a devil in hell who did not lay his lash on me on my way to purgatory." Many stories were told of ostensibly good men who went to hell because they had neglected the discipline, and their brethren had to assemble and flog themselves mercilessly to get relief for the dead soul.

It is, in fact, not so much the extent of self-flagellation that engages our attention until the rise of the Flagellants as the extent to which priests and confessors lay the lash on offenders of every class, even bishops, nobles, and princes, and often before the crowd at the church door on Sunday morning. One of the grievances of the Greek Church or one of the reasons it gave at this time for refusing to form one communion with the degraded Roman Church was that in the west there was a brutal custom of inflicting a heavy flagellation on a man before he was released from the ban of excommunication. Let me admit that the Greek Church was in most respects just as degraded as the Latin, but it seems that the Greeks had one feature of their pagan ancestors still to some extent: a dislike of the brutality of the lash, though it was by no means unknown amongst them.

In Europe, where the bishops, abbots, and Papal delegates shed excommunications over the landscape as freely as they shed blessings, even kings and nobles had to submit to the lash unless Papal policy advised leniency. Notable is the case of King Henry II of England whose knights murdered the archbishop of Canterbury, Thomas a Beckett. Some years ago I unearthed—it is, it is true, published in the Migne Collection but is always either overlooked or deliberately ignored by historians—the last letter of the archbishop. He tells a friend that he has no grievance against the king: that it is rival English prelates who persecute him and seek his life. However, it suited the Papacy to charge the king with murder and excommunicate him; and as part of the penance to obtain absolution he had to submit to be publicly flogged on his bare back by the monks of Canterbury. Many years later another Henry, the jovial Henry IV of France, incurred excommunication. But the Papacy, which applies its principles with inflexible rigor, now found that the king could do penance by proxy; and the two proxies, who got off lightly, were later made cardinals. A noble in the reign of Edward I was, for taking a nun from her convent—which was a terrible thing, but frequent—flogged at the church door on three successive Sundays. There are other cases in France. But they were not always so cruel. In Rheims when a new bishop was once to consecrated, it was found that by an oversight he had not resigned his earlier appointment. He had to bare his back before the cathedral chapter, and the dean gave him a "sound flogging." But it was all brotherly, and they fell upon each other's necks with tears of joy.

Flagellation as a punishment of offenses against either civil or ecclesiastical law was now more common than washing, but there was also a considerable growth of self-scourging. In the absence of a serious and adequate work on the subject and in view of the frivolity of most of the older works which we have we find historical writers and encyclopedia articles giving the public most misleading ideas of the practice at this stage. The work of reference to which any serious reader would look for sound and full information is the *Encyclopaedia of Ethics and Religion*. Unfortunately the editors seem to have obstinately believed that clerical contributors would tell the truth even when it was opposed to the church version of history. In describing the events which led up to the flagellation manias of the 13th and 14th centuries, to which I am leading up in this chapter, the writer on the Flagellants, after rightly observing that the early Christians indulged little in the practice—he most improperly tones down the extent of it from 600 to 1050—offers this singular explanation of the outburst in the 11th Century:

As the spiritual values of asceticism became impressed upon the consciousness of Christians in the 10th and 11th centuries men who burned with a passion for holiness of life resorted to flagellation as a means of subduing "the soul's evil yoke-fellow," the body.

It is sufficiently nauseous to hear a modern theologian use this language, but it is amazing to find him suggesting that the Fathers of the

Church and the Desert were not alive to the spiritual values of asceticism and that these were at last perceived in the most debased period of European history, the 10th Century. The plain fact is that at the close of the Dark Age an intense religious belief was combined with the lingering barbarism of the earlier period when men of robust peasant extraction, gross ignorance, and raw tastes were entrusted with power.

Damiani found that for a few centuries the bishops had in this respect been toning down the gross practices of the early part of the Dark Age. This was in part the work of a few educated and sober-minded prelates, who told the penitents that they might recite the Penitential Psalms instead of fasting or other physical penances. In large part, of course, it was not so admirable. It was just that giving an "alms to the Church" instead of fasting was more comfortable all round. To Damiani—I imagine him a gaunt, red-headed, fiery-eyed creature in a ragged tunic—with his terrific sense of sin and a clerical world saturated with sin all round him, this was outrageous. Folk must use the scourge: the old type, three twisted leather thongs on a short wooden handle end—if you really meant business—bits of wire or nails in the ends. He drew up a scale of benefits. Instead of reciting a single psalm you need to get or give yourself—preferably get from the clerical doctor —1,000 strokes of the lash. If you give yourself 15,000 it was as pleasing to God as if you recited the whole Book of Psalms. If you were heroic enough to rise to 200,000, as Damiani's friend Dominico Loricato had done (he said), you wiped out the penalties due for a hundred years of sin; and who wanted more than 50? This last is, of course, not the good cardinal's language. He put it that these 200,000 strokes, taken in successive doses, were equal to 100 years of any sort of penance. As to health, Damiani and his monk-lieutenant put about the stories of the immense longevity of the champion self-scourgers which I have given.

I put on historical truth, the evidence for which I have given in several works, in frivolous language when I say that Pope Gregory VII, Damiani, and most of their G.Men (as we might call them) were quite unscrupulous liars. The Pope, who searched the scriptures for such texts as "Cursed is he that refraineth his sword from blood," says in one of his extant letters that there is not much harm in a lie told in a good cause. Dollinger has shown in a special historical study how the whole of this gang of truculent puritans, who had the largest share in creating the power of the Papacy, used lies and forgeries habitually. For such men it was easy to snap up, if they did not themselves compose, the wildest stories about the efficiency of flagellation. It was largely by means of these and by their sulphurous language about sinners and devils that they, as Damiani boasted, induced large numbers of the people, of every class, to scourge themselves or have it laid upon by the white hand of the priest. The latter was preferable as it added to that Fascist power of the clergy over the laity which it was their chief concern to build up. Theodore Dreiser said:

Assure a man that he has a soul, and then frighten him with old wives tales as to what is to become of it afterwards, and you have a hooked fish, a mental slave.

So the puritans hooked their fish in thousands. It was, as none say more emphatically than Hildebrand and Damiani, an age of general license and great cruelty, but the one in 10 or so who took the creed (the chief article of which was now hell) seriously took lustily to the whip. Damiani tells of a widow of noble rank who gave herself 3,000 lashes a day. A human element of rivalry helped. Fame spread as in modern times does the fame of the marathon-dancers who hold out longest or the man who can sit longest at the top of a pole.

Here is a sample of the kind of story Damiani and his friends circulated about the efficiency of scourging. You might say that it gave folk the tip straight from the horse's mouth. Granet translates it from Vincent of Beauvais, who takes it from Damiani:

The Archbishop Umberto tells us that in the monastery of St. Sylvester

24

at Urbino a monk died and the brothers chanted all night over the body. And when the mass was being said for him the dead man suddenly sat up. When the brothers gathered round he began to blaspheme God himself, and spit at the Crucifix they offered him, and insult the Virgin Mary, saying: "Why do you chant and pray for my soul? I am in hell, where my lord Lucifer has crowned me with a crown of burning brass and dressed me in a cloak of brass . . ." The monks, therefore threw off their clothes, flogged themselves, and beat their breasts.

Of course, the dead monk now declared that he was saved and after admitting that all this fuss was because he had committed the sin of fornication and concealed it in confession, he lay down again quietly as a good corpse ought to do.

Another story comes from Geraldus Cambrensis (Gerald of Wales), who was at the time a devout prelate on the border of England and Wales and on the whole rather a decent fellow. He writes:

> In the north of England, in the church of Hovenden, the rector's concubine carelessly sat down on the tomb of St. Osanna, sister of King Osred, which had a wooden cover. But when she wanted to rise she found that her bottom stuck to the seat. The people crowded round, and she tore off her clothes and stripped and flogged herself till the blood flowed, weeping copiously. Then she was miraculously released.

One story was of a Junoesque type of nun who soundly thrashed the devil. One night the other nuns heard a terrible noise in the cell of Sister Cornelia Juliana. They found that she was flogging the devil and trampling him underfoot because he had come to tempt her.

Many modern religious writers seem to be concerned in all this orgy of stupidity and brutality with the question whether the man or woman who was flogged by the priest or another, especially in public, was or was not nude; then they talk about straining at a gnat and swallowing a camel. There was, of course, no general rule. Abbotts and abbesses confronting an offender would seize any sort of weapon—a stick, a poker, or a chain—and lay about the culprit without stripping. St. Bridget and others would flog with a bunch of keys. Often it is expressly said that the victim was stripped above the waist only. But those who contend that the victims were never or rarely nude know neither the evidence nor the gross mental outlook of the Middle Ages. The ecclesiastical historian Du Cange quotes this description of a monastic flogging from one of the more cultivated writers of the early Middle Ages, Matthew of Paris:

> Stripped of his clothes he entered the chapter and received the discipline on his bare flesh from his brothers.

There were, of course, theologians of the time who attacked the stripping—mainly because they would use any argument to discredit Damiani and flagellation—and the vehemence with which the friar-cardinal and his colleague and lieutenant, Cardinal Pullus, defended nudity under the lash shows plainly that they recommended it. This stripping was, they said, itself an important part of the penance.

But as I said, these folk are totally ignorant of the manners and morals of the Middle Ages. In our age of appeasement large numbers of people have been induced, by carefully selected and neatly dressed stories about him,, to admire the founder of the Franciscan order of friars, Francis of Assisi. Amongst other things they learn that in the early group of friars, there was a half-witted peasant, Brother Juniper, whom in his kind-heartedness the saint greatly favored. But these modern writers do not repeat the following story about Juniper which the Abbé Granet takes from a work of piety (now suppressed) written by the friars:

> He arrived one day at the city of Verona. Halting at the gate, he took off his drawers and wrapped them round his head (like a turban) and he wrapped his tunic round his neck. He then walked naked through the streets to his convent, the citizens handling him very immodestly.

As the friars wore no boots and stockings, or anything besides the brown tunic with linen drawers underneath that was then the costume of an Italian beggar, the friar was stark naked from the neck downward.

Another saint of the time, Robert of Arbrissel, a strict archdeacon of Rouen and doctor of theology whose ascetic life was offensive to both the clergy and the monks, retired from the wicked world into a rural district, and his fame for virtue was such that he soon had 5,000 nuns and thousands of monks following his rule. One of his communities had 900 nuns, and some of them were put over the monks; and it is expressly charged in some of the best writers of the time that Robert often slept with one of the nuns as "a new sort of martyrdom," as Abelard calls it. I do not at all suggest hypocrisy, but the fact shows ideas about modesty that would raise the hair of our modern saints.

Or take this story from Bernardinus de Bussis, pious author of a work in praise of the Virgin, *Opus Mariale*, from which (Sermon VIII) the Abbé Granet elegantly translates it. The date is near the end of the Middle Ages and it therefore shows the persistence of the same grossness. I should explain that the doctrine of the Immaculate Conception of the Virgin, which the modern Catholic thinks to be so ancient and authentic, was still in the 16th Century a matter of most violent dispute, and sometimes of blows, between the rival schools of theologians, and one day in the open square before the church a professor of divinity used disrespectful language about it in the presence of a lusty friar:

> He (the friar) laid hold of him and threw him over his knees, for he was very strong. Having then taken up his gown, because the man had spoken against the Holy Tabernacle of God (the womb of Mary) he began to lash him with the palm of his hand upon his huge breech (literal translation "his squared tabernacle"), which was bare, for he wore neither drawers nor breeches . . . Then a certain female devotee exclaimed, saying: "Mr. Preacher, give him four more slaps for my sake." Another presently after said: "Give him four more for me." Then another or a number of others, so that if he had attempted to grant all their requests he would have had nothing else to do for the whole day.

Bernardinus adds that it was probably the Virgin herself who directed the friar to perform this virtuous act.

Granet, by the way, a cleric with a spicy sense of humor, subjoins to this story one that he found in a French work, *L'apologie pour Hérodote*, of which the author said that he heard it from a lady of Lorraine who was an eye-witness. A preacher had almost exhausted the horrors he could think of in his sermon on hell, and he ended by saying: "It is as horrible as the arse of the bell ringer of this parish." "Which saying," Granet continues, "he uncovered the posteriors of the latter, who had placed himself there for that purpose, and had agreed with the priest to act that farce with him." Granet supports this with a story of a medieval friar-preacher who had made a bet that he would make the people laugh and cry at the same time. His pulpit was in the middle of the church, and he had so fixed his gown and pants that he could let them down. He did so in the middle of a serious part of the sermon and pretended that he did not notice, so that one half of the congregation wept at his words and the other roared with laughter at his naked stern.

To come back to Damiani's time, though I wish the reader to understand that this grossness lasted until modern times, our writers of lives of the saints do not give this detail about the life of St. Edmund of Canterbury. It is told with great pride in the virtuous Latin work of Claude D'Espence (*De Continentia*) of the 16th Century. The future saint was a young man studying theology at Paris about the year 1240 when "a young woman, daughter of his host,, often solicited him and, though he always repulsed her, persisted. So he invited her secretly to his study, stripped her, and flogged her. Many later saintly persons were fired by this noble example to pretend to the women who tempted them that they were ready for business until they got the chance to use the lash. St. Bernardine of Siena prayed to God for counsel when a woman tempted him. The saint's biographer says:

> God presently suggested to him to tell the woman that, since she would

absolutely have it so, she must strip off her clothes. To this the woman made no objection, and she had scarcely done it when Bernardine exhibited his whip, which he happened to have with him, and laying fast hold of her, he began to exert it vigorously, nor did he give up the castigation until her lustful arder was extinguished.

The chronicler naively adds that she loved him more than ever. At a later date I will give worse—or, if you prefer, better—stories of this ardor of virtue, but for my part I like better the story of the famous French poet of the early Middle Ages, Jehan le Meung, who in his *Roman de la rose* says that every woman is a whore. Whereupon the ladies of the court (who were all loose), had him seized for a flogging. He craftily submitted that he was guilty and asked as a favor that the lady who felt most deeply offended should first take the whip. There was no flagellation.

CHAPTER V. FIRST OUTBREAK OF THE FLAGELLANTS

The word flagellation at once suggests to the minds of readers of general literature a remarkable and extensive organization of men and women in the 13th Century for the purpose of self-scourging. Various reasons are assigned for this morbid phenomenon of the Flagellants in an age when Europe had touched about the height of its medieval civilization, the school movement had culminated in the appearance of the universities, wealth had enormously multiplied, art was flowering rapidly under the genial sun and rain of the new wealth, the serfs in most places won their emancipation, and large numbers of cities won their independence and often formed republics. The idea that one finds in Catholic literature, that belief and character were purified of the early medieval grossness at the same time, is a monstrous perversion of history. Just in that 13th Century the Inquisition had to be established by the Church and great skeptics like Frederic II and Manfred were amongst the most brilliant rulers of the age; while in regard to morals it will be enough to quote the verdict of a Positivist and therefore not anti-Papal historian, J. Cotter Morison, that the 13th Century was "an age of violence, fraud, and impurity such as can hardly be conceived now." That, I have shown elsewhere, is the verdict on it of all the leading historical authorities on each country.

On the other hand, the notion that this fanatical outburst was caused by the swoop of a foul and deadly pestilence, the Black Death, upon Europe is quite wrong. The articles in *Encyclopaedia of Religion and Ethics*, which I have already criticized, here again gravely misleads the reader. The writer, who is supposed to be an expert in church history, says that the Plague was the final stimulus to the birth of the Flagellant organization, which began in the 13th Century. There were two Flagellant movements or two periods when a perfect mania for public and collective self-scourging spread over a large part of Europe. The first, with which I deal in this chapter, was in the 13th Century and had nothing to do with an epidemic of disease. There is no notable appearance of pestilence in the medieval history of the 13th Century. When the Black Death did appear, nearly a century later, and stung folk to fanaticism, there was already the previous history of the Flagellants to give direction to their thoughts.

The truth is that religious writers were trying to preserve their fiction about "the beautiful 13th Century." The age which saw the rise of the great cathedrals, the old universities, the new and glorious art, and the orders of friars—we must not mention the Inquisition, the persecution of Roger Bacon, etc.—must, they say, have been an age of happiness as well as virtue. Catholic readers gather from their oracles that all that the world needs today is to return to that golden age. And the plain truth, which is not contested by any serious writer on the first Flagellant movement and is emphasized by all those Catholic chroniclers of the time from whom we learn the facts, is that the cause of the movement was precisely the deep and general misery of the age. As I have said that it was a time of general sexual freedom some of my readers may conclude that it cannot have been so miserable but one of the points I wish to impress is that when we speak of the 13th Century as vicious we are speaking of something more important than sexual matters. It was a time of incredible cruelty, of tortures such as we have seen revived in the concentration camps of the late war, of gross dictatorships, of repulsive perfidy and bad faith, of almost universal violence and injustice. There were journalists and essayists in the late war who lamented that we had got so far from the Age of Chivalry. *On the contrary, just what had happened was that we had returned to it.*

Every contemporary writer points out that one of the chief causes of this general misery in Italy, where the Flagellants first appeared, was the feud of the Guelphs and the Ghibbelines, or the Papalists and the Imperialists. The creation of the Holy Roman Empire by the Pope in the year 800 had been followed by four centuries of bloody strife of the Emperors and the Popes and was more savage than ever in the 13th Century. Dante's *Inferno* is a reflection of it. Families and cities were divided by such hatreds that the stories of individual outrages and cruelties seem to us not incredible. And what the modern religious writer is most anxious to keep from the notice of readers is that in that first half of the 13th Century the Emperor, Frederic II, was the finest man in the whole series and the most enlightened monarch in Europe, his son and successor Manfred was an equally accomplished humanist, while three Popes in succession, men who were not fit to clean their boots, waged against them a war that disgusts the modern historian and at the time completed the misery of Italy.

This explains the neurotic explosiveness of the Flagellant movement, which, it should be understood, affected only a small minority of the population: the one man or woman in a hundred who was nervously unbalanced and ready for collective hysteria. The form it took is explained by the ascetic development which I traced in the last chapter. But it is necessary to bring this up to date before I describe the epidemic. The monks, we saw, had introduced the practice of collective self-scourging as well as community-flogging for all sorts of offenses, and Damiani and his puritan crusaders had induced large numbers of the pious laity to scourge themselves or submit to the lash of the priests. New monastic or semi-monastic bodies arose in the 12th Century, and periodically zealots arose in the old orders who persuaded a few of the monasteries or nunneries to return to an observance of the rule, which now always prescribed a regular use of the "discipline" by the monks two or three times a week and a confession of offenses before the community once a week and punishment of all but the lightest offenses with the lash. In most monasteries and nunneries these rules were ignored or became mild formalities. The monks themselves made up stories about them; such as that of the abbot who noticed that a few of his monks disappeared occasionally, and he traced them to a basement of the abbey where they kept a store of choice wines and good cheer. The story is that he joined them in the orgy, only to get evidence, and next confessed it all in the chapter and had them all severely flogged.

As so few folk seemed able to observe the solemn vows they took, an order of women (Beguines) and men (Beghards—said to be the word corrupted to the English "beggar") who took no vows but lived in a community under strict rules was founded. A branch of these at Paris struck off on the usual plea that the order had degenerated, and these Turlupins, as they were called, were accused by their brethren of holding nocturnal assemblies in the dark in which they expressed their joy by adopting the costume that Adam and Eve wore before the Fall. It probably meant that they stripped for discipline. From them descended the Adamists, who are more positively charged with a close imitation of Father Adam. There were other new orders (Celestines, etc.) and all used the lash, but my purpose requires only that I speak of the two famous orders of friars that were founded at the beginning of the 13th Century and are supposed to give it a particular fragrance—they never bathed anyway—the Franciscans and the Dominicans.

Francis of Assisi, on whom quite a number of books have been written even in our century, was one of those fanatics of a poor ororder of intelligence in whom a violent asceticism dispenses with the need of character. Modern works on him are, of course, carefully expurgated. To say that he used the lash is a mild tribute. His particular lady-follower and saint, Clare, was just as sedulous with the whip, and she imposed it upon the body of Franciscan nuns which she organized. But

I am more interested in an early follower of Francis who is still popular in the Church as St. Antony of Padua. I confess that I have myself still a warm corner for my old patron saint (though none whatever for Francis), but he was surely great on the lash, and in a good cause he was once punished with it. This Franciscan order, the modern histories of which are grossly untruthful, was corrupt even before Francis died (1226), and Antony was scourged for opposing the corruptors. What concerns me most here, however, is that one of his early biographers claims that he inspired the Flagellant movement. This writer, quoted by Waddington, the leading Franciscan historian, says that Brother Antony's sermons were so moving that it was upon hearing them that "men began first to flog themselves in companies and sing hymns in processions. This custom, starting from so great an author, increased and spread all over Italy." Dr. Forstemann, author of the best work on the Flagellants (*Die christlichen Geisslergesellschaften*, 1828), thinks that this is not improbable, but the evidence for the beginning of the hysteria of 1260 is obscure. What is clear is that the Franciscan friars, or such of them as retained their original ardor through the first half of the 13th Century, kept alive the Dominican zeal for self-flagellation and stirred large numbers of the laity to practice it.

The rival body of friars, the Dominicans, did even more. Francis had called his body "Brother Ass" and treated it accordingly. Dominic took as dark a view of it as did the ancient Persians, who believed that the devil had created it, and treated it ferociously. He was, like Ignatius of Loyola, one of the darker and most fanatical type of Spaniards, carrying all the fierceness of a soldier into the exercises and service of religion. The modern religious person who cannot believe us when we say that every page of history testifies that these medieval folk really believed their creed yet were, in the mass, extraordinarily licentious, cruel and violent, imagine them listening every Sunday to moral exhortations from the pulpit as he does. They, of course, did nothing of the kind. Preaching was not a routine custom in the medieval church. Hence the enormous success (for a few days or weeks) of the fiery zealot who came to a town, preceded by rumors of his wonderful preaching, and called the people together, often in the meadows outside the walls.

Dominic founded his order for two purposes: to detect and punish heretics and to provide preachers. Hence it was that his friars almost monopolized the work of the Inquisition, which was founded at this time. He would have an offender stripped to the waist and flogged through the streets from the gate of the town to the church door. His friars had Count Raymond of Toulouse, leader of the Albigensians and one of the best princes in France, so savagely flogged, when the Pope's "crusaders" made him powerless, that he could hardly dress himself and limp from the church to his castle. The laity were urged to flagellate themselves for their sins as the friars did, and the fraternity produced some powerful preachers. One of them, John of Vicenza, in 1233, got, the chroniclers say—but take a pinch of salt—a vast audience of 400,000 in the meadow outside Veroma (and no mike!) and wrought them up until they forswore all this Guelph and Ghibelline business; until the Ghibellines perceived that he was just a Guelph agent of the Pope, and they drove him back to his monastery.

In short, by the middle of the 13th Century the idea of self-flagellation was as familiar as taking salts in the morning is today and the practice was extensive, apart from the monasteries and the jails. Couple with this the fact that, as every writer of the time points out, the people of Italy were racked with suffering and anxiety. Frederic and the monstrously cruel tyrant Ezzelino had recently died but Manfred had assumed power and in the late '40's there was a great Ghibelline (imperialist) victory. The general mind was in a state of dangerous tension, and many predicted that the end of the world was near. Life in Italy was comically different from what Catholic writers now represent, and the worst strain was in parts where the majority adhered to the Pope and echoed his scandalous attacks on the fine-minded Manfred.

Such a part was the city of Perugia, where the flagellation mania broke out. Who inspired it, or if any one man did inspire it, is uncertain. Our knowledge is based upon a score of local chronicles, often of the crudest description, and these are usually based upon rumor. It is now usually said that one of the great Dominican preachers, Rainerius or Raniero, fired the people. While one report was that it was miraculously started by a baby in its cradle and others said that it was a spontaneous movement of the people, it seems that, seeing the excitement of the people of Perugia, some hermit or ascetic named Raniero, not a Dominican monk, went to the city and began to preach there. It is probable enough that he was one of the self-flogging school and recommended that form of penance to the distracted citizens. The winter had been severe, food was short, and the warring armies, of which every soldier had the license to rob, rape, and murder, might descend upon them at any time.

It was in these circumstances that the first Flagellant movement appeared. Long processions of men and women filed through the streets day and night. At first the clergy headed them with a crucifix, and the banners of the Guilds were borne before them. They were naked to the waist—this I, take it, was a gradual development—and they lashed themselves with leather whips until the blood flowed on their backs and shoulders. Nobles and burghers and their wives and daughters mingled with the lower citizens and peasants. Boys down to the age of five, naked to the waist like their elders, walked two by two through the streets lashing their little shoulders and piping the melancholy chants about their sins. "Repentance and Peace" was the slogan, and we may substantially accept the assurance of the chroniclers that hundreds laid aside the bitter feud with their neighbors and began to lead lives of virtue. All profane songs and every variety of dance and entertainment ceased, we are told; in fact, one bold chronicler says that assassins offered their daggers, hilt first, to the men they had intended to kill. Everybody knows how revival services do effect these temporary reforms and we may broadly accept the picture. But "it was a momentary exaltation of the emotions, not a reform of morals," Forstemann says, and he is not a hostile critic. In this epidemic of the 13th Century we hardly find any suggestion of irregularities, as we do in the 14th. But the chroniclers, who are all pious enthusiasts, would scarcely mention such things, and we must use our knowledge of human nature. There were plenty of irregularities in the old revivalist meetings in America.

At first unquestionably the Flagellants were sincere to the point of fanaticism, and their fame spread over Italy. Large bodies of them set out as missionaries for neighboring cities, where the entire population flocked to see them. Where the Ghibellines were in power the gates were closed against them; and they had a mixed reception at Rome. In other cities the bishops and his clergy met them at the gates, and often the Podesta (mayor) and chief citizens joined in the flogging. It was now winter, but snow, slush, and mud did not interfere with their rule to halt and flog themselves severely twice a day. "Hermits left their groves and came to the cities to preach," one chronicler poetically writes. In many places the doors of the jails were opened and prisoners joined the folk. But there were sober critics who began to murmur. This unorganized migration of thousands of fanatics caused great difficulties in regard to food, and the exposure to the rains and snows was tempting providence, and—at last we hear—men and women of the wrong character are joining. The clergy also began to be alarmed. The sacraments of the Church, administered by the priests, were the proper way to get forgiveness of sin. They must confess to a priest—this was now a law of the Church—and leave it to him to appoint the penance. In short, the novelty wore off and people hungered again for the fleshpots. By the spring of 1261 little remained in Italy of this first epidemic except a group or fraternity of Flagellants here and there who would keep the tradition alive until the next great outburst.

Meantime processions had crossed the Alps from the north of Italy, and the mania spread to Austria, Germany, Bohemia, Moravia, Hungary, Saxony, and even Poland. They met in most places a good deal of opposition. Their fame had had time to spread all over Europe, and probably the prelates had consulted Rome. Most of them, and such princes and civil magistrates as were docile to them, frowned on the movement and either forbade the pilgrims to enter the region or at least to perform their antics in church or in any street where there was a church. Still the fanatics ploughed on through the snows, for it was still the later part of winter. The account usually given confuses this movement of the 13th Century with that of the 14th and gives it more success in Europe than it had. A Polish chronicler says that when they reached Poland "they were all burned as heretics." In parts of Germany, the local historian says, "the sect was destroyed by fire and sword." It had become an anti-sacerdotal movement: a fight of the system in which a man could save his own soul and the Roman system in which the priest was indispensable. Not much is said of this in the pious chroniclers but we may be sure that the Flagellants retorted with strong language about the morals of the priests, monks, and nuns. They were comprehensively bad, as the ecclesiastical historian Hauck shows as regards the German lands. The movement was over by the summer of 1261.

One point of some importance may not occur to the reader. No antiseptics were known in those days, and there must have been some heavy suffering amongst the tens—taking the whole period and range we might say hundreds—of thousands who scourged their backs and shoulders until the blood flowed. Ointments which had a certain virtue were known, but we may doubt if these fanatics, proud of their scars, would use them. We must remember also the filth of the time. The days of the great medieval public baths had not yet arrived, and they were in any case open-air summer baths, while this development was in the winter when few even of the rich took baths. There must have been a horrid lot of disease as well as deaths and suffering from exposure.

And it was all as futile as the man-devouring crusades of the previous century. The Papacy itself ended the century with a Pope who is admitted in the most severely impartial of modern histories, the Cambridge History, to have been "doctrinarily a skeptic" and a man for whom "the moral code had little meaning." He was followed by the scandalous Pope of Avignon, of the great Schism, and of the Roman Renaissance. With short periods of better men the Papacy entered upon three centuries of degradation. The general state of the Church—prelates, priests, monks, nuns, and laity—may be imagined. No one of the religious writers who praise the 13th Century ventures to suggest that it laid the foundations of a better moral or social world. They just take advantage of the fact that there was progress in various departments of life to ascribe this to religion. There was progress in art, knowledge, industry, trade, wealth, and law. Of all this the flagellation movement was a flat denial, a gesture of contempt. But that there was any rise of the general standard of character, any reduction (except in short local spasms) of the mighty volume of crime, violence, perfidy, and injustice no serious writer suggests. And since by morals our modern apologists mean above all things sex morals it is enough to say that there is not one of them who does not admit that the ensuing period, the Renaissance, was sexually the loosest in European history. Their only defense of the Papacy is that the world had become so corrupt that it corrupted even the Popes.

CHAPTER VI. THE FLAGELLANTS OF GERMANY

It is admitted by historians that the power of the Papacy and the Catholic hierarchy reached its highest point by the year 1300. The few "great Popes" of the preceding five centuries, relying upon that general and crass ignorance that had enabled them to use a large number of forged documents and had reduced man to a state of peculiar docility by a general acceptance of the doctrine of hell, had created a sacerdotal power that had hitherto been unknown in history. It is an ironic comment on the excuse that is made for these Popes, that they sought only the good of man and felt that the end justified the means, that just in that year, as I said, the power was held by a man who, as proved by Roman clerical witnesses, scoffed at the fundamental articles of the faith and said that adultery was as innocent as washing one's hands. This was determined by the greatest law court in Europe and is admitted by every candid historian. At his death it transpired that the whole "Sacred College" was corrupt, and the new Pope sold the Papacy to France and shifted his court to Avignon. That city soon became the most infamous in Europe: so vicious that the picture of the life of the higher clergy which the great Petrarch, who lived near it, has left us would be incredible if it were drawn by any other man.

Italy now had a new affliction. The streams of gold that had hitherto poured into Rome from all parts of Europe were now diverted to Avignon and the Papal capital fell into a state of dire poverty and decay. In the rest of Italy the old violence and perfidy were sustained and, while some cities had the wealth to maintain the advance of art, there was a great deal of misery. In view of this a Dominican friar tried in 1334 to revive the practice of collective self-flagellation. He was a fiery preacher of the old type and drew, it is said (with the usual generosity), crowds of 4,000 to 5,000 hearers. They saw flames issuing from the holy man's throat when he preached, and a broad halo of light enveloped him. He soon had long processions going with him from town to town. They wore white coats or tunics, colored mantles with the sacred lettering J.H.S., white stockings, and leather jack-boots. They had a staff in one hand and a scourge of knotted cords in the other and flogged themselves. "Peace and Mercy" was again the slogan; and, the chroniclers say, the flowers of virtue again sprang up in their path. But we will not linger over this. The monk took a body of his pilgrims to Rome and was laughed out of the city. He took them to Avignon, and the Pope, not a bad sort though he is the one who is said to have given occasion for the proverb "Drunk as a Pope," condemned him, and the great crusade fizzled out.

A few years later another epidemic of piety broke out in Italy and the whips sang merrily once more. This time the leader was a beautiful and virtuous maid, and we are told that on one occasion 10,000 folk gathered round her in a meadow outside Cremona. This was really too much. It had been bad enough for laymen to encroach upon the privileges of the clergy but a woman. . . . The clergy found, they said, that the "saint" was the mistress of a wicked and designing priest. The Inquisition had her arrested and proposed to burn her at the stake. But some gentlemen, whom she doubtless rewarded, set her free, and she and the movement disappeared. But in 1347 something far worse than remorse for sin and hunger fell upon Europe and inspired the second Flagellant movement.

Most readers will not need to be reminded that this was the Black Death or the Plague, now fairly identified as bubonic plague. Starting

Flag.

from China, where is slew many millions, it oozed across Asia to Turkey and the Levant (the Mediterranean coast of Asia Minor). Here the Venetian and Genoese vessels gathered to bring oriental goods to Europe, and their crews back to the ports of North Italy not only a harrowing story of a mysteriuos scourge but the germs of the disease. The great trade route at that time was to Austria, Hungary, and Germany. It passed on to France and England, and, in short, in three years the Plague slew about one-third of the entire population of Europe or, it is estimated, about 25,000,000 men, women, and children. Villagers flocked to the towns to get the more powerful protection of the great shrines or crowded round the large abbeys. The new and splendid cathedrals were thronged. In short, they did everything possible to spread the Plague and the continent became one vast charnel house. In numbers of towns and cities every second person died in appalling agony. Such was the state of medicine that quacks sold pills that were in part compounded from the bodies of victims of the plague. The chroniclers say, that there were also earthquakes, cyclones, and floods. The cry of end of the world rose again.

Here was the material for a greater religious panic than ever, and so Europe witnessed the second and greater episode of the Flagellation. Where it started there is no definite evidence, but most writers, finding one chronicler after another saying that it began in "Old Germany," conclude that it probably spread from Austria, Hungary, or South Germany. It reached as far as Poland in the east and England in the west; and, of course, it backfired into Italy. But it was essentially a German movement, and Forstemann hardly notices it anywhere else. Its early stages we do not know. In all descriptions we find it organized with what modern writers call German thoroughness.

Putting together the accounts by different contemporary writers and ignoring local variations, which were bound to occur, we get a picture something like the following: A town is apprised that the Brothers of the Cross are approaching along the country road, much as a provincial town is still excited by news that "the circus is coming," and large numbers stream out of the gates to meet them. Winding along the lane is a procession, two by two, of 200 men and women (sometimes up to 500) with their heads and faces hidden in cowls, a captain and two lieutenants leading them, chanting harsh and doleful hymns about sin and repentance. The dead cattle stink in the fields and dead animals litter the roads and streets. But the soldiers of the cross—they have a large red cross on their garments back and front, though all their clothes are filthy from lying in the mud—march sturdily on behind a banner of fine purple silk. Entering the gates of a town they make straight for the church. One or more lie down at the door extended in the form of a crucified. A brother lightly and symbolically brushes them with a whip, saying, "Rise, for your sins are forgiven." In the church they sing their own litany, one of their better singers leading, for in this movement everything is organized. Then they march to the public square or market place, which is probably before the door of the church, or, if it is a village, to a nearby field. Here the big ceremony begins.

Surrounded by a crowd of spectators, they take their stations in a ring or circle, strip themselves (both men and women) to the waist, retaining only a linen cloth or skirt that reaches from the groin to the ankles. They pile up their outer garments inside the circle, and the townsmen often bring their sick and place them in the circle. In one town a dead child is hopefully put in. They chant, and at a given signal throw themselves to the ground, lying full length in the posture of the crucified. Of snow, slush, or mud they take no notice; and, although this would not seem to the medieval chronicler a detail worth mentioning, there was absolutely no sanitary service in those days, and the streets and squares, several inches deep in stinking dust in dry weather, were covered after rain with a thick carpet of filthy mud. Again at a signal they rise and begin to flog themselves to a rhythmical chant from the choral leader. The scourges are three or four leather thongs fastened on a wooden handle or thick twisted cords through the ends of which two short nails, sharpened at both ends, have been driven, so that the points stick out about half an inch. These points often stick in the flesh from the fury of their blows and have to be torn violently out in order to keep time. Blood streams down shoulders and backs, and the nude breasts of the women and girls heave. They prostrate themselves again, then rise and resume the flogging. Finally—we imagine them panting round the circle—one of them with loud and distinct voice reads out, to the amazement of townsfolk or rustics, a copy of a letter which an angel, the radio post of that age, brought from heaven to Jerusalem on December 25, 1348, in which Christ and his Virgin Mother sent a sort of Christmas greeting to the holy Brothers of the Cross and assured them that this was the way to atone for sins and escape the pit. They put on their clothes and march in couples back to the church.

These 200 were pilgrims or missionaries, giving this gory performance three times a day—morning, afternoon, and (by candlelight if necessary) night—and once extra when a brother or sister died, then appeal to the townsfolk to form a local branch of the brotherhood. Any one wishing to enter must make a general confession (of all sins committed from the age of seven), swear to do the thrice-a-day flagellation for 33 and one-third days (in honor of the years of Christ's earthly life) and get the permission of husband or wife. He or she (generally she, it seems, from the accounts) must abstain from meat and from carnal intercourse during that time, not speak to any person of the opposite sex, and eat all meals in silence. In that year, from the summer of 1348 to the middle of 1349, when Europe was one vast stinking plague hospital, there was a ready response everywhere. In the cities thousands took the cross, and the missionaries marched all over Germany, crowds often streaming out into the country to greet them.

The religious idea was repulsive enough in itself, and against the month of virtue and meekness which it effected in thousands of cases we must put the fact that the fanatics caused one of the worst massacres of Jews in the history of that unfortunate people. It is said that in one German city, Mayence, 12,000 were killed. They were tortured and burned, locked in their houses or synagogues and fired. Catholics say that the Pope intervened mercifully in favor of the Jews. The Jewish historian Graetz admits that he did, feebly and almost futilely, but only when the Jews paid him a large sum of money for protection. This Pope, Clement VI, was the gayest sybarite of the Avignon series of Popes, but we will return presently to his character and his action against the Flagellants.

It seems clear that the violence against the Jews started from honest fanaticism. They had killed Christ. But they were soon linked with the more pressing and obvious evils of the race. By a sort of anticipation of the Protocols of the Elders of Zion it was said that they were taking advantage of the misfortunes of Christendom to gain political power over it. They had poisoned the wells and streams and caused the epidemic. Naturally there was no need to destroy their property, and looting began, as in recent Nazi years. Loot became as important as religious zeal, and many joined or pretended to join the Flagellants, as they had joined the Crusaders, simply in the hope of plunder. One chronicler says that in some places bandits joined the brotherhood so as to get entrance into a town and they then produced their arms and took over the town. It was an age still of general banditry (chivalry) in the country, and even small towns were walled and the gates guarded and closed at dark. In most of them the houses were of timber, and some were burned down when the Jewish houses and synagogues were burned.

What other irregularities there were in the Flagellant movement it is difficult to determine. In contrast to the movement of the 13th Century, when most of the contemporary notices were respectful, the chroniclers of the 14th Century wrote at a time when the movement was branded by the Pope and generally considered a damnable heresy. They hint at evil things but the heresy itself was so monstrous a thing that it is not clear that they mean anything more. The Pope in condemning them speaks of "base things" (*turpia*), in language that generally refers to sex, but considering the state of his own palace and town we are not particularly interested in what he did mean. The most important passage—just a sentence—is in the work which the famous and pious French lawyer Gerson wrote on the subejct. After a long attack on the heresies of the Flagellants, he says: "I say nothing about the thefts, the raping, the adulterers." He was, however, particularly referring to a later outbreak in Spain which we will consider later. Several writers accuse them of extorting money while the majority tell us that they were strict in that respect: that brothers were forbidden to ask even for hospitality and that on entering the fraternity they had to pay only four cents, which even in modern coinage was not equal to half a dollar. Probably there was graft in the later stages of the movement.

Moral grounds had almost no place in the formal condemnation of it, and we wonder how far the suggestion of some modern writers, that the semi-nudity of the women must have led to a good deal of looseness, is justified. To the sexologist who knows how flagellation is used in some cases to stimulate the feeling of sex, it is an interesting question what the effect was of this mass-scourging. There is practically no evidence. On the general description, the movement seems to have been so strictly organized and so open that lapses must have been rare. But in the later months we see ground to suspect the human element. The letter from heaven must have been well known to the leaders to be a forgery. Credulous as medieval folk were, there were numbers who denounced the letter. In these later months too the leaders claimed to work miracles and drive out devils. Baronius quotes from an unpublished manuscript in the Vatican library that in some places the troops took about with them and imposed upon the public a number of girls, who at the meetings professed that they had been delivered of devils. We generally find that sex is not far away in such cases. On the whole, however, the evidence suggests that the numbers of the brotherhood who went from town to town were as genuinely ascetic as the Damianis, Dominics, and Antonys whom I have already described, and there does not seem to have been much chance of hole-and-corner business. Most of them seem to have been the sort of folk who if one lash caused a wicked thought would promptly give themselves 10 more. The semi-nudity of the women was, as I said, no stimulating novelty to the Middle Ages, as one may gather from the painters and sculptors.

The movement was crushed because it was based upon a vile and most poisonous heresy: the theory that you could get your sins forgiven without the assistance of the Church and could be even more sure of getting the pardon. At a fairly early date in the movement this set the brothers and their leaders in opposition to the clergy; and as it is a simple historical fact that most of the clergy were corrupt and most of the bishops at least sensual, the feeling of superiority grew stronger. The famous letter from heaven was almost an order to folk to prefer these ascetics to the sensual or depraved clergy and monks. The Flagellant idea, in fact, cut at the roots of the entire church system, which had now become tremendously profitable to the prelates and the Papal court, and it must be destroyed. The Inquisition had been established for just such a purpose.

The people themselves naturally grew tired of the grisly novelty in a few months, especially after the plague had swept over a district and was not likely to return, and the churchmen were encouraged by this to take the field. A band of the Flagellants, apparently ignorant enthusiasts who did not know the facts, ventured into the Papal city of Avignon, "the new Babylon" of Petrarch's letters. The Pope, Clement VI, had recently bought the city and a good stretch of territory round it for the modest sum of $50,000; but as Queen Giovanna of Naples, to whom it had belonged, wanted a lenient absolution for being involved in the murder of her husband and permission to marry his murderer, the Pope was able to strike a good bargain. Petrarch may be too poetical when he describes Clement as "an ecclesiastical Dionysos with his obscene and infamous artifices," for Dionysos of Sicily had been a monster of vice, but the Pope was unquestionably an epicure in whose palace the ladies of the nobility, the chief of whom was said to be his mistress, had much more power than monks had. We can imagine the quivering of the dainty Papal nostrils when these muddy and glassy-eyed fanatics appeared in his city.

The chroniclers say that the cardinals restrained him from taking violent action against them, but read Petrarch's description of the elderly goats who formed the "Sacred College." Clement wrote at once to the kings of France and England, the Emperor and the leading German archbishops and sternly—we have his letters in Baronius—condemned the movement. As a result they were unable to get a footing in France and England. A company of 120 of them reached London from Belgium, but they were greeted with ridicule and abuse and forced to return to Belgium. The kings of France and Poland enforced the condemnation, and the heretics were soon crushed in those countries. In Germany and Austria the struggle was fiercer, but the archbishop had a powerful weapon in the fires of the Inquisition, and by the end of 1350 the movement was in ruins.

That is to say, the organized movement, defying the clergy and affirming that flagellation was the appointed way of salvation, came to an end. But the idea was, as usual, merely driven underground. Large numbers of the faithful in various countries continued to believe in the efficacy of the scourge, and there was no reason in Church-law why they should not use it in private, provided they had confessed their sins to a priest. How individuals, fanatics or frauds, tried occasionally to revive the communal flogging we shall see in the next chapter, but the famous movement which is mentioned in all European history is that of the Flagellants of the 14th Century passed away with the plague. If you dared now to say that to flog yourself for your sins until you bled was more likely to earn forgiveness than the magical formula of a hypocritical priest you were a heretic, and the world was full of Inquisitors (which means "Searchers" for heresy). The Franciscan friars had not left a monopoly of zeal to their Dominican rivals. As the property of the condemned man was divided between his accusers, his judges, and the authority, such zeal was profitable, and to give the least ground for suspicion—the victims were often completely innocent—was dangerous.

It is hardly necessary to add that the fanatical movement, like that of the previous century, left no enduring traces on the masses that had admired the Brothers of the Cross. Italy was in a worse state than ever. The free republics or cities of the 13th Century became—if I may use a modern term—Fascist dictatorships of the most terrible type. The counts, dukes, and marquises who founded dynasties in them were generally cruel and licentious, often phenomenally cruel. The people were infected with the spirit of cruelty, and incredible stories of social behavior are found in the contemporary historical writings. With the Pope far away on the borders of France and the evil fame of his court spreading everywhere the clergy as a body were not encouraged to be virtuous. When the Papacy was recalled to Rome the fight for the tiara was so fierce that the Church was rent by the Great Schism, at least two Popes, often three, and mostly men of inferior character when they were not criminal adventurers, shooting anathemas at each other during nearly 40 years. And a terrible cloud was threatening Europe like another plague from the east. First Timur (or Tamerlaine) seemed about to conquer it, then the Turks, with ebbs and flows, spread over the Greek world and church, and it seemed to be only a question of time before they would sweep over decadent Europe and, as folk conceived, vent their pagan lusts and savagery on Christendom.

CHAPTER VII.   SPURTS OF FLAGELLATIONISM

In recent years there has been a "swing to the Right" amongst American writers on European history. In the last century, or the second part of it, when history began to be critical and scientific, nearly all the authorities were either skeptics or Protestants, and they described the medieval period with considerable frankness. In the present century Catholicism has become a political force in America, and beyond question this fact has been reflected in the writing of history. I personally know a publisher who commissioned the writing of a historical work and instructed the author to select his material in such fashion that Catholic censors would not get it excluded from use in colleges, which would restrict circulation. Some of the minor professors of history have completely falsified the record of medieval life and incorporated in their works the modern Catholic version, which even judged by the older Catholic writers, is thoroughly mendacious. It seems less innocent but is equally fatal to sound education that some of the more reasonable professors have claimed that we must now apply our modern psychology to the study and this compels us to take a new view of "the mind of the Middle Ages."

In recent psychology there is no such thing as "mind" much less a mind of a whole continent during several hundred years. Psychology demands no change in the writing of history. It is the psychologist who has approached the angle of the historian. He studies behavior wherever he finds it, and if he is faithful to the authentic documents he is chiefly impressed by its bewildering variety and contradictions. The writer who sets out to appease Catholics (and get a better circulation) finds it perfectly natural that in such a pious age whole populations should bare and lash their backs until the blood flowed. But if you turn to the work of some real authority on Europe in the Middle Ages and read of the amazing extent of vice—of cruelty, perfidy, injustice, and unchastity—you see that the picture is somehow out of focus.

The truth is that even at the height of the three Flagellant movements—we have a third to consider, though heavy flagellation is a much less conspicuous element of it—the scourger was not one in a hundred of the population of Europe, and such social influence as the movement had died away in a matter of weeks. Not a healthy rooted conviction but collective hysteria was the source of the more striking manifestations. Thus the best modern Catholic historian, Dr. I. Pastor, says of Italy when the third Flagellant movement appeared—and it was sincerely supported by immensely larger crowds than the two preceding outbursts—that "the prevailing immorality exceeded anything that had been witnessed since the 10th Century" and "cruelty and vindictiveness went hand in hand with immorality" (*History of the Popes,* I 97). And this refers to behavior in the age immediately following the terrific manifestation of piety and penitence in 1399.

The whole period is not one of simple and deep piety, but extraordinarily complex, shallow, and shifting, and the reader will not forget that here I am studying a single feature of it, though it is useful occasionally to sketch in the background. The self-flagellators were in fact more logical than the clergy, and their conflict with these was far from virtuous. The clergy taught folk that to prevent or to atone for sin "the flesh" must be mortified and put before the images and pictures of saints who had considered the lash the chief instrument of such mortification. The great saints to the Italians of that time were Francis and Dominic, Antony and Bernardine, and to throw any doubt on the virtue of the scourge seemed almost an insult to them.

Hence the idea of self-flagellation continued to burn in the minds of the pious few, and they knew that it was still officially imposed upon every man in the two orders of friars and practiced wherever a friary did not share the general corruption. In spite of the standing Papal condemnation, local groups of flagellants often appeared. We find the archbishop of Cologne in 1353 making this complaint and threatening the offenders with excommunication. Four years later it appeared again, and in 1360 much wider attention was drawn to it. In Thuringia, in the heart of Germany, Conrad Schmidt announced that he had divine orders to revive the Flagellant movement. He was, he said, the prophet Enoch, who, you will remember, was taken up to heaven in the flesh and had been spared the usual painful process of getting there. God, he said, had sent him back to earth to restore the esteem of the lash. As to these ecclesiastical pronouncements, he said, they need take no heed of them as all power had now been transferred to Conrad himself. The clergy threw a practical doubt on this claim by burning Conrad and 90 of his disciples at the stake, and the movement was crushed.

Some writers observe that the heresy next appeared in the Turlupins of France in 1373. The chroniclers tell with a shudder that these were followers of a man named Turlupin who said that as God in making our first parents had made no clothes for them, nudity was divinely appointed. There is no reason at all to include these heretics with the ascetic self-scourgers. If we may believe the contemporary writers, in fact, they were simply free-love communities or just the opposite of the dour folk who tore their backs to atone for sins of the flesh. Unfortunately in such matters the chroniclers are apt to make the wildest statements. They connect the Turlupins on the one hand with the Beghards (mentioned in the previous chapter) who were most probably pious and virtuous critics of clerical morals, and on the other with the Waldensians, who were certainly ascetic early Protestants.

I am, however, inclined to recognize that these Turlupins were just nudists. One of their leaders at Paris was a woman—the usual "beautiful young woman"—named Jeanne Debanton, and poor Jenny was burned alive by the Inquisitors in the Pig Market, near the St. Honoré Gate. There were two later nudist movements in that century. One lot, the Bohemian Adamites, made their Eden inoffensively out in the country, but even this shocked the clergy, and the imperial cavalry were sent to cut them up. Their ideas spread to England and for some years had followers there. Their main idea seems to have been that as God made the equatorial organs as well as the mouth there was not the least reason to be ashamed of them. The third group, the Picards of Belgium and Germany, learned from their prophet Piccard, who said that he was the son of God sent to teach men a wiser mode of life, that nudity and free intercourse were part of the original divine plan.

The real interest of these things is incidental. I have already pointed out that the age had no more delicacy about indecent exposure than we have about legs. If anything, the freedom was greater than ever at this time. I have not space here for lengthy explanations and must refer the reader for the evidence to my large *History of Morals* or *History of the Roman Church,* (both published by Haldeman-Julius). But I must point out that just this period of the Biblical nudists was the golden age of open-air bathing in central Europe, the reminiscence of which is preserved in the names of so many South-German towns (Baden, Weisbaden, etc). Hundreds of thousands flocked to these open-air baths in the summer, and the freedom of life was such that the Pope's secretary, Poggio Bracciolini, one of the most immoral writers of that age of erotic writers, wrote an enthusiastic description of the baths. In the open, it is true all wore a sort of loin-cloth, but there were plenty of private baths with no restriction, while the brothels were as abundant and open as beer shops. The sexes mingled freely, and priests, monks, and nuns, many of whom spent a long summer vacation there regularly, frolicked in the shallow ponds with the laity. But when heretics appealed to the legends of the Bible to justify nudity they had to be exterminated with fire and sword.

The next Flagellant movement occurred in Italy in the last year of the century, but it was possibly an offshoot of a Spanish movement which we will examine presently. The chroniclers surpass themselves here. Some put its origin in Ireland and some in Scotland, some in England, Spain or Germany. There is evidence of such a movement in 1398 in Savoy, and it may have reached there from Spain, but what we definitely know is that self-flagellants appeared again in May, 1399, in a small town near Turin. Life was still one of affliction, for the feuds were still bitter and bloody, the Papal Schism still raged, a vile type of criminal ruled the Pope in Rome, and now the shadow of the Turk was approaching from Asia. As before, in 1200, prophets put the end of the world in 1400. They were, as before, crusaders. They wore long white linen tunics with hoods (and eyeholes) that were drawn over the head and face, and so that you might, if you desired, distinguish the sexes—though they insisted on a rigorous separation—the women had a red cross on the hood and the men on the shoulder. Jesus Christ and his Virgin Mother had, they said—they had a long and circumstantial story about this—appeared on earth and ordered them to revive the flagellant movement but now in complete accord and cooperation with the clergy. They marched through the towns two by two or three by three in the old style, but now usually with priests at their head chanting melancholy hymns, especially the *Stabat Mater* ("The Mother stood beside the cross"). They made the church their center in every place, sleeping in it at night, and after nine days of devotions they moved in procession to the next town.

But the movement never defied the clergy, and its practices were not as grisly as those of the earlier movements. We do not read of bare shoulders and backs, and blood is never mentioned. Most of the contemporary accounts say that at the close of a service they "did penance," and one account assures us of the meaning of this by saying that "they whipped their shoulders." It appears to have been a fairly humane process: doubtless like that observed in such friaries as paid any attention to the discipline. A knotted cord, not armed (as formerly) with nails or wire, and laid on over the clothes is not a painful exercise. I had to do it twice a week for years.

The interest of the movement is mainly in its prodigious success. There seems to have been no outstanding preacher to fire the people, yet we read of 10-, 15-, or even 20,000 folk joining in the processions and services. From the first the cry that the end of the world was near gave a powerful impetus to the movement, and presently the rumor spread that the holy brothers and sisters wrought miracles. They touched the sick with the crucifix which they bore at the head of the procession and forthwith the blind saw, the dumb spoke, even some dead rose again. After a month or so they had five crucifixes in the procession each of which had a record of miracles. Then there was the moral miracle. We need not doubt the assurance that in the full flood of the popular hysteria enemies were reconciled and all sorts of sinners mended their ways—for a few weeks. Cardinal Baronius says in his history that the whole thing lasted only two or three months. It seems to have been four or five months from the first appearance of the Brothers of the Cross or of Penance in the north to the complete and almost sudden collapse of the movement under the Pope's ban in Rome.

While it lasted it formed a notable page in the history of flagellation. It was summer and was no hardship to saunter, chanting, along the Italian lanes, halting at crossroads to edify the crowd of villagers. At night they slept, the women and children apart from the men, in chapels and their courtyards and the grounds of monasteries. There is no rumor of scandals. By the time they reached Genoa the clergy and monks joined them, nobles and their wives and daughters walked in the ranks, the narrow streets were crowded. Even the archbishops welcomed them. The wicked Duke of Milan would not admit them to the cities of his dominions, and they turned south. The cry ran before them that the *Bianchi* (Whites) were coming. At Bergamo, 6,000 folk put on white robes and joined in the services and the novena ended with a torchlight procession through the streets. Report said that they numbered 10,000 by the end of August, 20,000 a week later; nobles and commoners, rich and poor, priests, monks, and laity marching together with 40 beautiful banners, chanting their *Stabat mater* to the austere old music of Jacopone da Todi. Even across country they marched a thousand strong, and everywhere the clergy and the civil authorities turned out to receive them. At the great city of Bologna, we are asked to believe, the whole population put on the white robe and at the end of the novena marched out to Imola. The merchants of Venice would not receive them. It was bad for trade, they said. Florence gave them 14,000 citizens to support them. So through July and August the enthusiasm grew until, at last, doubtless with some trepidation, they approached Rome.

There were many now who scoffed, but at first it seemed as if they would capture Rome. The great Count Colonna carried the crucifix at the head of the procession, and many other nobles were in it . A crowd of 15,000 Romans gathered to receive them at old St. Peters, and the Pope blessed them and exhibited to them one of the great treasures of the church: the cloth on which the face of Christ, covered with sweat and blood, had imprinted itself when he was being led to execution. But the Pope and his cardinals were, the chronicler says, uneasy. It was still the age of the great Schism, and Pope Boniface IX wondered if there was not some dark plot of the rival pope at Avignon in this extraordinary invasion of Rome. And they brought no money to Rome. That may sound to some an ungracious remark, but Rome was sodden with greed and every other vice. It was just preparing to receive pilgrims from half of Europe for a "Jubilee," at which the Roman and Papal officials would break the record for theft, rape, and murder. Writers who tell you of the tens of thousands of white penitents and say nothing about the normal condition of Rome and Italy are constructive liars. The Pope called an assembly of the cardinals to discuss matters and no one knew what to do, but just then, according to the contemporary writers—and one of them in Rome at the time was a sharp German lawyer in the Papal service, Dietrich of Neheim, who tells us this as well as the sins of the Popes—something happened that greatly relieved them the court.

At the head of the procession as it entered Rome the miraculous crucifix was borne by a tall, dark, bearded man whom the Whites called John the Baptist. He probably pretended to be a reincarnation of that prophet, as another leader called himself Elias. He had set up his cross in a church and said, "Work a miracle," and several drops of blood came from the side of the crucified figure. There were at the time hundreds of these fakes; bleeding Christs, weeping madonnas, liquefaction of the blood of martyrs, etc. The Papal officials sent experts to examine the cross and, of course, they discovered the trick. Some say that the man squeezed the blood out of a secret cavity. Others say that he coated it with wax and exposed the cross in the sun so that the blood would flow. Under the gentle attentions of the Inquisition the man then confessed that he was a Jew (others say an apostate priest), and he was piously burned and the whole vast movement melted away like hoarfrost when the sun rises. Italy slipped back into vice and violence as easily as it has risen to a week of virtue, and Rome, under the infamous Cardinal Cossa, who was then the Pope's Vicar and practically ruled the Church (of which he would soon be Pope) cheerfully gave its mind to new plans of corruption.

But in that same year self-flagellation had found a new champion, one of the greatest saints of the age, a confessor of Popes and Kings, a Dominican monk and even Inquisitor. This was the Spaniard Vicente Ferrer, now in high honor in the calendar of St. Vincent Ferrer. As I said, the dilemma of a pious mind was that most of the great saints of Italy during the last four centuries had been terrific self-flagellators, all the monastic orders were supposed to practice it, and councils of the Church had repeatedly prescribed it for the punishment of sinners, especially in the south of France and north of Spain where Vicente lived and studied. In four years of the 13th Century (1212-16) three great councils had repeated the prescription. It was quite common to see a man come forward with bared back and a scourge in his hand during the mass on Sunday morning and be lashed by the priest before the whole congregation. It was not uncommon to see a man who was still under public penance, possibly after a recantation of a mild dose of heresy, included in a religious procession and flogged by the priest at every crossroad. Saints being just logical Christians, who drew elementary practical inferences from their creed, Vicente, like so many others, reasoned that if the lash was the recognized punishment for sin it was a good deed to lay it on your own shoulders.

In 1398 he became a wandering preacher, and for 20 years he traveled about Spain, France, and Italy—he even visited England at the king's invitation—preaching to the usual vast crowds, which were swollen into tens of thousands in the mind of the chroniclers. They do not explain the little difficulty that Vicente spoke only Spanish and a little bad French. Doubtless that was a small matter in an age when the general piety was rewarded by daily miracles. His converts clung to him and soon he had processions of men and women chanting the usual dirges and lashing their bare shoulders. They pushed on through rain and snow and frost, but none of them (we are told) was ever ill. In short, flagellation went on as merrily as ever over a large part of Europe.

The Inquisitors were embarrassed, Vicente was one of the chief ornaments of their own Dominican fraternity, and he was greatly honored and esteemed by princes and cardinals. On the other hand, poorly concealed remnants of the old heretical Flagellators were being detected every year, and self-flagellation was apt to raise a suspicion of heresy. The great French lawyer Gerson wrote to Vicente and urged him to drop the pagan and indelicate practice and leave folk to take their penances from the priests. He would not, and, as a great Church Council was to meet at Constance in 1414, some of the theologians decided to appeal to it.

It is one of the many ironic pages of the history of the time. The main object of the Council of Constance was to end the great Schism by deposing all three Popes, especially the Roman Pope, who was one of the most versatile criminals that ever wore the tiara. The list of his crimes and vices drawn up by the Council includes all the major sins in the prayerbook. And if we are disposed to be impressed by the fact that nearly 500 cardinals, prelates, abbots, etc., met to perform this laudable act, one of the best chroniclers of the time tells us that more than 1,000 prostitutes also were attracted to Constance for the duration of the Council, and the Emperor who presided over it was thoroughly and cheerfully immoral. Vicente seems to have been summoned to give an account of his work. He got a cardinal and two theologians to represent him instead, but the question does not seem to have been discussed. They were busy damning the Pope—and they put an almost worthless and easygoing man in his place—and John Hus. It was this new Pope's secretary, Poggio, who went off to the German baths when the Council was over and wrote a glowing acount of the pleasant life there. As to Vicente and his thousands of followers, they just disappear form the European stage. Vicente died soon afterwards, and the great edifice of virtue he had built up melted away in the usual fashion.

CHAPTER VIII. THE AGE OF ART, PIETY, AND VICE

Probably in no other century of history was so much noble art produced as in the 15th Century. No one of its creations could, of course, rival the Parthenon of ancient Athens, but Athens was one Greek city and the Parthenon was one building in it. Italy in the 15th Century was superb with art, though Rome had not risen to the level of the rest of the country until the close of the century. Painters and sculptors of historic importance were found in all other cities, goldsmiths and metal workers did superb creations, and every city seemed to be clad in velvet, silk, and brocade. Great cathedrals appeared, and the nobles and merchants raised magnificent palaces. Culture returned to something like its pagan splendor, and even science was ardently cultivated in northern cities. Yet I do not know a competent historian who says a good word for that century in any respect except art and letters. In western Europe medieval barbarism lingered, the Italian artists giving the name Gothic (or barbarous) to the architecture of which the English and French were most proud. As to morals, the less said the better. Even Catholic historians like Hilaire Belloc speak with contempt of what was to prove the last century of a real Catholic (universal) church.

I leave it to artists and cultured folk to explain how the race could rise so high in those respects yet incur so much disdain from general historians. As far as our special subject is concerned, we are prepared to find a strange variety of phenomena. The public self-flagellation which we considered in our last chapter was always apt to lapse into heresy. Not only did the priests regard with suspicion every attempt of the people to find the way of salvation without their assistance but men and women who chose the hard manner of life were naturally prone to reflect upon the morals of the clergy. The enormous majority of the priests, monks, and nuns who filled Europe were fat, lazy, sensual, and dissolute. The attempts of the modern writer to rebut this by discovering a saint here or a strict monastery there only confirms the general truth. We shall see how, when its appalling losses drove the Papacy in the next century to put its house in order, half a dozen new monastic bodies had to be founded, so hopeless was the task of reforming the older bodies.

In these conditions the old type of heretical or anti-clerical flagellation still flourished, but it was driven underground. In the year in which the Council of Constance was supposed finally to suppress it, the Inquisitors declared that they found it flourishing extensively in Bohemia. It took the usual form. They were Brothers of the Cross, and they persisted in holding that the famous letter from heaven ordering this "baptism of blood" instead of the Church's sacraments was genuine. Their leaders were burned, and even those who recanted and were for a time in jail were decorated with a blue cross, scourged by the priests, and despised by most of their neighbors. The Dominican friars, who willingly ran the Inquisition for the Church, were always looking out for them, and a batch were burned every few years. We have to bear in mind that this was one of the birth-pangs of Protestantism in Europe.

The real religious history of Europe is vastly different from what one reads in so many American manuals. Instead of the people being solidly devoted to their Church and their feudal rulers—if you can attach any importance to the feeling of a population that was to the extent of at least nine-tenths illiterate and densely ignorant—there was from the year 1100 onward a spirited attempt to throw off the yoke. From the political angle there was a considerable fight for democracy and on the religious side a mood of rebellion that took sometimes a skeptical form (Abelard, Frederic II, the general run of the Albigensians, the witches, etc.) and at other times an evangelical or Protestant form (Waldensians, Beghards, Hussites, Wyclifites, etc.).

The self-flagellation movement was one of these Protestant developments, though it got curiously mixed up sometimes with what seemed to be a totally different movement, unless it is the chroniclers who confuse them. In 1446, for instance, the Dominican monks, who are responsible for more religious murders than any other organization that ever existed, reported that Crypto-Flagellants, as they were now called, were once more numerous in central Germany. I gather from the records that the monks bribed peasants to betray these nocturnal meetings in cottages in which profoundly religious men and women used to scourge themselves. They found a dozen in one small village, 14 in another, and so on. They met on Fridays and took a particularly stiff dose of their medicine on Good Friday. From the records it is clear that this was the old movement that had retired underground but was still strong. . Some of the accused testified that they had kept up the practice for 30 or 40 years. They had learned it at the age of 14 or 15 from their mothers or grandmothers. Some carried it so far that they flogged their babies soon after birth. Many died for their faith, protesting that this was Christ's wish, not membership of the corrupt Church.

Yet there were further large disclosures in 1453, 1454, and 1456. The creed was evidently still widespread in the villages of Thuringia and on the slopes of the Hartz Mountains. And here we get in the chronicles a curious mingling of the Christian penitentical idea with Satanism. A chronicler says of the trials in 1453:

. **Man and wife, brother and sister, went together to a house and prayed there, in the cellar, to the devil. He came in the form of a bee (BUMMEL) and touched them all on the mouth. It was very meritorious to yield to him. Then the lights were extinguished, and they grabbed hold of each other and sinned with each other, whether mother, sister, or daughter. These heretics were burned all over the country.**

Except that I never elsewhere read of the devil (really the priest of the local group) coming in the form of a bee—he generally entered in the dark in a goatskin with a stone or horn organ—this is a rough description of the witch ritual, but the chronicler professes to be describing the trial of Crypto-Flagellants. Other writers on the trials say that "some prayed to Lucifer."

It would be a quaint development if the stern sect of the Flagellants did get mixed up in places with the diametrically opposed sect who held that there was no such thing as sin to be atoned for. In one of my Little Blue Books I have given an account of witchcraft. The common idea, still occasionally endorsed by some writer who has not got beyond the old fairy-tales about the Middle Ages, that the witches were morbid or mischievous old women is as ludicrous as the fable that folk once lived for hundreds of years. Witchcraft was an organized cult of the devil, a religion to those who practiced it, and it counted its adherents, who were of all ages of both sexes, and every rank and grade of culture, by the million. But its teaching was the exact opposite of the Christian ethic or any form of asceticism. The essential psychology of it is that whereas folk had for centuries professed the Christian theory of sex but in practice acted as if sex were the richest gift of life, it was time to drop the theory; and since this meant repudiating the authority of Christ and regarding him as an enemy of the race, it was more logical to worship Antichrist, the real friend of man, the beneficent spirit that defied the Christian God. Thousands cheerfully died for this faith; millions were put to death for it. The only historian who ever laboriously tried to compile the number of witches put to death between the 11th and the 18th Century said that it was at least 9,000,000. It was a European religion, and the essence of it was joy in sex, particularly in the orgies of the nocturnal meetings, at which priests and nobles, learned doctors and officials, aristocratic ladies and refined young women, occasionally joined the people.

I must refer the reader to whom all this is strange to any account of the movement. I just note here that it was one of two reactions to the paradox or muddle of the Middle Ages. A small minority were driven to ascetic or expiatory exercises of which self-scourging had become the chief type. The witch movement was a pragmatic reaction and, being profoundly heretical, it was fiercely persecuted not only by the Inquisitors but also by the Protestant leaders when these appeared. It is difficult to imagine a mixture of real flagellation and Satanism, and I am inclined to think that some chroniclers have confused the two different types of nocturnal meeting or that in some cases the Inquisitors have put the Satanist formulae into the mouths of self-flagellators and in the agony of torture they repeated them.

Of the ascetic self-flagellation there is not much trace after the collapse of Vincent Ferrer's movement. The discipline was prescribed in the rules of the Franciscan, Dominican, and other monastic bodies but they were generally demoralized—of this we have the emphatic assurance of the prelates at the Council of Trent in the 16th Century—and it would be only an enthusiast here and there who would take the rule seriously. There is a story of one similar to the story of Bernardine of Siena which I told in an earlier chapter. Brother Matthew of Avignon, Capuchin friar, was on a begging tour in Italy, and he received pious hospitality in a castle in Piedmont. The beautiful daughter of the noble family pressed Brother Matthew to accept hospitality of a kind that was inconsistent with his holy character and when he refused, went to his bedroom at night. The old translation of the chronicle runs:

> The Saint having been charitably received in a certain castle in Piedmont, where he was then begging about the country, a young lady, extremely lonesome and of noble birth, came during the night, stripped to her shift, to visit him in the room that had been assigned to him and, approaching the bed in which he slept, solicited him to commit the carnal sin. But the holy friar instead of answering her took up his discipline (scourge), made with the usual well-knotted Spanish small cords, and flagellated her so briskly upon her thighs, her posteriors, and her back, that he not only made her blush with shame but left upon her skin the bloody marks of his violence. . .

The last sentence indicates that he removed her one garment. It is, as I showed, nonsense to suppose that folk were particular about nudity in those days. And it is also clear, since she evidently took it for granted that a friar would welcome her approaches, that Brother Matthews was an exceptional type, and a serious self-flagellator.

There was one more attempt to extend the practice of self-scourging to the laity, and, although it falls in the 16th Century, it was not connected with the rise of new monastic or semi-monastic bodies with which I deal in the next chapter. Carlo Barromco, whom American Catholics know as St. Charles Barromeo, was a nephew of one of the "worldly" Popes of the 16th Century. He was converted to ways of virtue by the premature death of a brother and was confirmed in those ways when a bastard son of one of the cardinals and three companions went with poisoned daggers to the Vatican to finish the Pope. Although Protestantism was sweeping Europe the Papal Court was almost as foul as ever. However, an ascetic monk ascended the Papal throne, and Charles, who had become Archbishop of Milan, restored the flagellating fraternities in his city. Long processions of men and women, clothed in long linen robes and with red crosses on their foreheads, trod the ribald streets of Milan on the church festivals and at funerals. They had knotted girdles and before the procession started each brotherhood met in its own chapel and the members flogged themselves severely (but apparently not on nude backs and shoulders). The idea became popular, and rival brotherhoods distinguished them-

45

selves by the colors of their robes like the charioteers in the ancient Roman Circus. There were white, black, gray, blue, red, green, violet, and brown penitents.

The practice spread to other cities. Rome at one time, when a strict Pope held power for a few years, had no less than 100 of these picturesque brotherhoods and sisterhoods. Not many years earlier the gayest sights of the city of Rome had been the passage of cardinals, armed or in hunting dress, attended by troops of horse, or the most beautiful courtesans of Europe taking the air in their carriages and receiving the homage of nearly every prelate they met. Now for a few years they were replaced by the processions of the flagellators—not very violent and certainly not gory, let me add—and the monks and nuns of the new orders. In little more than 10 years the penitents would disappear and the gay ladies, who made immense fortunes out of the prelates and nobles, return to gladden the heart of Rome.

We will come to that period presently. Before we leave the 15th Century we wonder whether in such an age we can find any trace of erotic flagellation. We saw that there are faint traces of it in antiquity, and we shall see that there are much more numerous traces of it in modern times. The moralist or preacher will say that as the 15th Century came nearest to the conditions of the ancient pagan and the modern pagan world we are likely to find the practice. When he means, as he generally does, that the preceding part of the Middle Ages had been too religious and docile to the church ethic to suffer such sordid developments we smile. There had been many virtuous individuals, even virtuous monasteries and nunneries, in Europe since the 4th Century, but there had never been an age of virtue, and the great mass of the people, lay and clerical, had enjoyed a remarkable sexual license. One is at times tempted to say that people had such inflamed impulses that they never needed recourse to sexual stimulations, but this would not be correct. From the church prayerbook and lists of sins we learn that there was a considerable recourse to aphrodisiacs or supposed aphrodisiacs—they are too gross to be described here—even amongst the peasantry during the time, the Dark Age, when Europeans had returned nearest to the robust animalism of their ancestors. As to "morbid" practices, the works of Damiani, to which I earlier referred, show that sodomy was tremendously rife in the 11th Century, as it was again in the 15th. It was, in fact, all through the Middle Ages. Five Popes were certainly perverts and several others reasonably suspected.

The psychology of erotic flagellation is, however, a question that we must postpone. Here I need say only that the feature of the 15th Century which seems most pertinent to my present subject is that it was remarkable for the erotic freedom of its more notable writers. Five out of six of the greater literary men of Italy—Lorenzo Valla, Poggio Bracciolini, Aretino, Ariosto, Machiavelli, Beccadelli, Filelfo, and even Pope Pius II in his earlier years, practically made a cult of sex or, as they boldly and repeatedly said, "the two Venuses." Some of them, and some of the cardinals, wrote comedies, often staged in the Vatican, in comparison with which the comedies of Aristophanes, Plautus, and Shakespeare are restrained.

We feel that behind all this there must have been a varied sex experience but although these writers not obscurely praise homosexuality and freely accuse each other (as well as princes, popes, and cardinals) of it, there are not many reliable sources of erotic flagellation recorded. One of the few strict writers of this time, Pico della Mirandola, tells us of one in his work *Contra Astrologos*:

> I know a man, still alive, of extraordinary and unheard-of lust. For he is never sexually excited until he is whipped, yet he wants it so much that he scolds the flogger if she is too easy and is not content until the blood flows ... The wretch begs this service most appealingly of the woman he frequents, and he gives her a whip which he has hardened by soaking it in vinegar, imploring the whore to flog him. As he is otherwise a decent fellow he recognizes and hates his disease.

. The man, he says, explains that he has practiced this since youth, when he learned it from other boys. This not only connects an early stage of Masochism with the custom of flogging in school but suggests a practice of some extent. That is, however, the only recorded case in the 15th Century, and I find only one or two for the 16th Century. Meibonius, the Dutch physician whom I quoted in an earlier chapter as specially interested in this matter, quotes it from Cardinal Rhodigianus:

Not many years ago there lived a man who had, not only the salacity of a cock, but a most incredible ingenuity: the more vigorously he was beaten the more ardent he became in lust. It was altogether a strange thing. You would wonder whether he liked the blows or the sex-pleasure most. . . He used to beg and pray to be whipped and used to soak the whip in vinegar on the day before he was to be flogged. If the whipper seemed to go more gently, he fell into a rage and abused her and was not satisfied until she drew blood.

The man gave the same explanation as is given in the preceding case: he had learned the practice in boyhood from other boys. As there is more than half a century between the writing of Pico della Mirandola's work and that of Caelius they clearly do not refer to the same case. Boileau refers vaguely to a case in an obscure medieval writer, Meugbus Faventinua, who mentions a man who used to have himself beaten on the loins with green nettles—possibly he had read the recipe of the ancient priest of Priapus—and Meibonius quotes his second case from some 16th Century "famous physician" whom he calls Otto of Brunswick, who says that at the seat of the Duke of Bavaria there was a man who could not have intercourse with his wife unless he was just flagellated. The Dutch physician adds from his own experience:

A certain citizen of Lubeck, a butter and cheese merchant, was brought before the magistrates for adultery and other crimes and was exiled from the city. A whore whom he frequented confessed before the judges that he could never commit the venereal act unless he was first whipped. The adulterer at first denied and then acknowledged this.

Meibonius is able in this case to give the names of the witnesses and full particulars.

Brantome, a French noble of the 16th Century, tells in his well-known *Memoirs* a story that may be put in the same category. A noble lady of his time, he says, was "not content with her own lasciviousness but used, further to provoke and excite herself, to have the most beautiful Dames and Maids of her court stripped and had great joy in looking at them. . . . She used to smack their bottoms with her hands, joking and roaring with laughter. If they committed an offense she would flog them with a stout whip. At other times she would just lift their skirts instead of stripping them, for they wore no trousers." Brantome adds that she "used to make the maids laugh or weep according to the circumstances." Doubtless there was a good deal of this mild form of Sadism in the private infliction of flogging that was then common. The language in which the tutor of Lord James, one of the (many) bastards of King James of Scotland—Cooper wrongly says James I of England—used to tell the ladies of the court how he chastized the young prince implies some such feeling. But we will consider later the question of flogging in schools which was a practically universal practice until recent times. In the Middle Ages it was by no means confined to schools, jails, and barracks. Any offender in a large house, even a chaplain or a friar, might be sent down to the kitchen to receive the lash in the appropriate part to the joy of the kitchen maids. It is said that the famous (St.) Thomas Moore had gentlemen of his suite flogged in his house.

Another type of flagellation that increased about this time and must be classed as generally erotic was a practice of confessors of imposing a flagellation on women penitents and insisting on carrying out the sentence themselves. A popular story of the time implies that this was common, though there are few references to it in the decrees of ecclesiastical conferences. The story is that a woman told her husband that her confessor had ordered her to retire with him behind the high altar of the church to be flagellated. The husband asked the priest to allow him to be the scapegoat as his wife was delicate. The priest consented, and as the man prepared himself for the sacrifice, the wife, who stood by, said to the priest: "Lay on heavily, father, for I have been a great sinner." We shall see a few famous cases of this sort later.

On the whole the evidence of erotic flagellation in the Renaissance period is small but it unquestionably implies that there was a widespread practice. The men, we saw generally, declared that they had contracted the practice in schooldays from other boys. It is an opinion largely shared by modern sexologists that erotic flagellation, either self-imposed or administered by others, commonly begins with experience while being flogged by a master. In the earlier part of the Middle Ages there were few schools, and in those which appeared, under the stimulation of the Spanish Arabs, after the 11th Century, there was a rule no personal relation of master and pupil and little discipline. Novices who entered monasteries did so in late adolescence or manhood. During the Renaissance schools approaching the modern type multiplied, and one of the first pedagogical principles was "Spare the rod and spoil the child." It clearly encouraged sadistic impulses in masters and would often reveal the erotic aspect of flagellation to their victims. But we will take these special types of flagellation later.

CHAPTER IX. THE REVIVAL OF PENITENTIAL FLOGGING

Of the three main uses of the lash, the penal, the penitential, and the erotic, it will be understood that the first, about which I have said so little, flourished exceedingly during the period I have covered. The penalties of the civil law were as gross as they had ever been in any civilization; indeed grosser, since they still, even in Papal Rome, included castration and other mutilations. Italian ambassadors to the Papal Court in the 16th Century speak of seeing men who suffered that mutilation for certain crimes—a Jew having relations with a Christian prostitute, for instance—taken round the streets bearing the organ on a pole. To this vast amount of brutal flogging that was done in the jails the Inquisition had added its tortures. A lash of the bloodiest type was one of the instruments of pious persuasion. But I assume that my readers are not interested in this type of flagellation. It will be enough to show later how it was maintained in penal systems, navies, penal colonies, etc., until the 19th Century.

During the period I surveyed in the last chapter, broadly from the end of the 14th to the middle of the 16th Century, there is comparatively little evidence of the other types of flagellation. The Catholic, of course, imagines the thousands of monks of the various orders— Benedictine, Augustinian, Cistercian, Franciscan, Dominican, etc.— torturing themselves with holy joy in the tens of thousands of monasteries that now studded the map of Europe, and too many manuals of the history of the Middle Ages encourage him in that illusion. The only generalization that it is safe to make about these freaks of the pious world is that the overwhelming majority of them were corrupt. The "new history" searches for recondite political or sociological causes of the Reformation that occurred in the 16th Century, and the historians are wasting their time or currying favor with Catholics. The Protestant rebels made it perfectly plain that they left the Church because it was corrupt both in doctrine and morals, and the Catholic authorities denied only the corruption in doctrine. No Pope from about 1450 to 1550 was really concerned about the moral corruption but there were a few strict cardinals and archbishops, and from these one can draw up a comprehensive indictment of the Papal Court and the Church, as I have done in my *History of the Roman Church*. As far as my present theme is concerned, it is enough to say that when the spread of the revolt compelled the Popes (who resisted for 30 years) at last to summon a reform council (Trent) the German prelates demanded the suppression of all monastic bodies on the ground that their comprehensive corruption was one of the chief causes of the Protestant schism. The Catholic historian Pastor quotes two Popes, Hadrian V and Pius V, declaring that the revolt was due to "the sins of men, especially of the prelates and clergy" and "the damnable and detestable life of the clergy." But I have given the full evidence elsewhere.

The other point which it is necessary to make in order to put the next outbreak of flagellationism in its proper perspective is that the claim of a Catholic Reformation or Counter-Reformation is false. The Council of Trent, which was to reform the Church in faith and morals, did practically nothing in the way of moral reform, which it excluded from discussion as much as possible. Two things happened. There was a reform party in the Italian Church, and it got three puritan Popes elected between 1550 and 1650. They ruled, collectively, for only 15 years, and while they were certainly zealous for chastity, they left other disorders so rampant that by the end of the 16th Century the Papal Court and the Church were almost as corrupt as ever.

The other consequence of the rise of a reform party under the stress of public scorn and Protestant revolt was the appearance of a new crop of fraternities and sisterhoods with a zeal for self-flagellation. Catholics themselves are often puzzled as to why these new bodies (Jesuits, Servites, Oratorians, etc.), living in communities under vows, must not be called monks. The answer is that, as I said, the reforming prelates themselves wanted the monastic orders suppressed, as inevitably tending to corruption, and would have no new ones established. Such men as Ignatius had to fight long, and hypocritically, to get permission to form a "society" (the Society of Jesus is the correct name of the Jesuit body). Other men and women by favor, bribery, or persistence got permission to found new "congregations," as they are technically called, and there was a considerable growth of new sisterhoods or bodies of nuns. Cooper has half a dozen chapters on these in his *History of the Rod,* but it is a world in which he moves impatiently and he is unreliable. He confuses the new and the old bodies of monks and nuns, and he often makes curious statements about them which I am unable to verify after considerable research. Cooper's (really Bertram's) book might be classed as a work of disedification or prurient entertainment, and as such it is admirable. At the British National Library (the British Museum) the copies of it are kept in what is officially called "the Cupboard," which is supposed to house obscene books, or marked "Table," meaning that a reader must remain under the eye of the officials if he is permitted to have a copy. It is, in fact, not an "indecent" book but it talks freely and joyously about those parts of the human anatomy which are providentially padded to receive flagellation.

In this new development of self-flagellation communities of men and women a leading part was taken by the fiery little Spanish lady who is remembered as St. Teresa; just as the fiery Spaniard Ignatius of Loyola founded the Jesuits about the same time. Teresa was the daughter of a Castilian noble and a pious mother, and she took to edifying stories, especially about the self-flagellating saints, so enthusiastically that at the age of 7 she persuaded her brother to elope with her and go to seek the crown of martyrdom amongst the Moors. Later she took up with equal enthusiasm the stories of chivalrous knights that had become as much the rage in Spain at that time as detective stories have in modern America. There never was an Age of Chivalry in Spain or anywhere else. Teresa, now in her puberty, devoured the stories, and on top of the stories of flagellating monks they gave her an emotional indigestion from which she never recovered.

She became a Carmelite nun at the age of 18, but for more than 30 years attracted no particular attention. The Carmelite order, for both sexes, was so old that its origin had inspired a vast amount of pious (a violent) quarreling. But like all the other orders it was in complete decay. What the convent at Avila was like we are poorly informed, but the story runs that about the age of 40—notice the connection with the change of life—the mild and acquiscent nun became a fierce ascetic and reformer and a transcendental mystic. Her fame spread over Spain and attracted the attention of the Inquisition. But holy men protected her from the gay-living Spanish clergy and the incompatible authorities, and the Pope graciously consented that Teresa and the few nuns who agreed with her, should set up a little house of their own and lash themselves to their hearts' content. Teresa had virtually founded a new order for she had not only restored the old Carmelite rule but added rigors to it, the chief of which was flagellation. The Pope approved this also. It is one of the little ironies of the time that this Pope and others who piously approved these new establishments of virtue were themselves "bad Popes" and permitted the grossest license in Rome.

A reform of the Carmelite monks also was carried out under Teresa's direction, and in these monasteries self-flagellation was ordered three times a week. Five degrees of faults were recognized, and for the heavier the monks were cruelly beaten on the naked back and shoulders or made to undergo all sorts of painful and humiliating penances. In the houses of women the discipline was lighter, but there was in each house a room with a store of birches, and the novice chose one. For faults—as to be found going to the kitchen, remaining longer in the toilet than a good nun ought (they had no baths, of course), etc.—a nun would be whipped three times before the whole congregation of sisters. For more serious offenses a nun might have to lie across the door of the chapel to be trodden on or appear lightly clad in the refectory. But I am interested only in the flogging. A nun had to ask permission to go beyond the prescribed austerity but, naturally, the example of Mother Teresa and the wonderful visions and wisdom and the fame her mode of life gained for her fired many to emulate her. We hear of a Carmelite nun in Italy who slept on sacks and flogged herself every day or got the other nuns to tie her hands and lash her severely. Others used hooks, chains, books, etc., with which to beat themselves. Some went mad, and most of them died young. Teresa herself, a woman of prodigious nervous energy, lived to be 67.

As the reform spread to other countries one is apt to think that at last we have thousands of men and women lashing themselves every day until the blood flowed. Far from it. When Teresa died, after 35 years of this sort of things and a reputation that spread all over Europe, her rule was carried out in only 17 convents of women and 16 of men, and there was already much talk of scandals and laxity. Teresa was one of the transient phenomena of monastic history . Most monasteries and convents in Spain continued to pick flowers by the wayside on their journey to heaven. The question has been raised by modern sexologists, in fact, whether Teresa's own life does not evince a good deal of masked sexual pleasure. Some of the figures in which she expressed her visions are held to have a sexual significance. The argument seems to me strained, especially as all these experiences—the experts do not seem to have noticed—come after the change of life, and Teresa had never been of a robust type. Modern study has, however, shown that we cannot draw sharp distinctions in the old fashion in such matters. The sadistic scourger or the self-scourger does not necessarily have a specific consciousness of the sex impulse, although it may count for a good deal in the general confused sentiment. The sex feeling may be sublimated or disguised just as other strong feelings, even of pain, may awaken the special nerves of sex life.

There had already appeared in France an aristocratic lady—there was not much chance for commoners to get anything from Rome unless they had powerful friends—who had established a new order or congregation of nuns with flagellation and other austerities. Jeanne de Valois was the daughter of Louise XI and for a time the wife of Louis XII. After the annulment of her marriage she got permission from Pope Alexander VI, the most flamingly immoral Pope of that age, to found an Order of the Annunciation, under the direction of the Franciscan friars who in later years greatly appreciated their control of the nuns. It was not crudely ascetic, though Cooper professes to have read somewhere that Jeanne put young nuns across her knee when they misbehaved.

A century later, however, an Italian lady, Maria Vittoria Fornari, either reconstructed it or got permission through the Jesuits, to establish a new Order of the Celestial Annunciades. Maria, a widow, had had a lot of trouble with the devil, who was always tormenting her; which is not an unusual experience of young widows. To defeat him she used to flog herself mercilessly until she fainted. For the sake of humility she lived amongst beggars, and her Jesuit confessor put her under the control of a peasant girl whom he directed to give her plenty of chastisement. Such women are apt to have visions in which they imagine that heaven directs them to get some particular form of devotion started or a new congregation established, and between this and a sort of sublimated vanity or ambition they spend years intriguing for this purpose. With the help of the Jesuits she got the permission of the Pope—again not a particularly religious man—to found her new congregation in honor of Annunciation.

Maria Laurentia Longa, another pious Italian widow of the time, founded the order of the Capuchin nuns. The Capuchins are one branch of the order that Francis of Assissi had established, but there was a schism amongst the brethren and much ink; and, apparently, some blood was shed over the question of the precise shape of the hood (capuche) which the saint had worn. They degenerated like the others but a fiery preacher of theirs reformed part of the order in 1525 and set the scourges flying merrily once more. Maria Longa, widow of a statesman of the Kingdom of Naples, feeling the temptations of widowhood, took to scourging herself severely like the good Capuchin friars. She would strip her shoulders and get others to lay on the lash. Cooper says that she used to lie on the ground and get someone to beat her with a tough stable broom; but I suspect Cooper of having had revelations from heaven, or the mahatmas, occasionally. At all events Maria decided that there must be Capuchin nuns as well as monks, and an obliging Pope put his golden seal to the decree, doubtless at the usual price.

The order was introduced into France by another royal lady, Louise of Lorraine. In the convent which she founded there were much beatings for the least fault that the city was scandalized. Yet women penitents of a certain type would have no relaxation of these practices; which doubtless encourages the suspicions of the sexologist about flagellation. When Jeanne de Chantal, a French widow and great friend of the famous Francis de Sales, founded an order, about the same time, in honor of the Visitation of Mary (by an angel), she and her director decided that they would have none of this slaughter-house stuff. If the nuns behaved as naughty children they must be treated as children: made to wear a fool's cap or a big and grotesque pair of spectacles, loaded with timber to look like an ass, and so on. Only in serious cases were they to be birched. But it did not work. For some reason, which may, as I said, interest the sexologist, a pious lady who is conscious of sin or afraid of the devil would rather be flogged on one or another part of her anatomy than be made ridiculous, and the new foundation failed.

Another congregation of nuns that did not favor the lash was the Ursulines, founded about the same time by the Jesuits in honor of the legendary virgin of Cologne. But these nuns were all teachers and therefore in an exceptional position. More severe were the contemporary Hospitalites who were often flogged on the bare back, and the Urban nuns, founded by a daughter of Louix XIII, who scourged themselves or were flogged until they bled. The Feuillants, another offshoot of the corrupt Cistercians, and bitterly persecuted by them, had the distinction, besides vigorous self-flogging, that they slept only four hours a night and ate on the floor. The Penitents, an offshoot of the Franciscans, were mothered by the Italian countess Angelina of Korbain, who, on the night of the wedding into which her father forced her gave her husband the satisfaction only of seeing her strip and scourge herself. He soon grew tired of this nightly entertainment, and she formed a community of ladies with the same peculiar ideas.

These women did not invent quite as many tortures as the fakirs of India but they seemed to have the same strange conviction that the holier you were, or the less you had to expiate, the more drastically you must treat brother ass. Many, of course, had the idea, which was as old as the Pythagoreans of ancient Greece, that fasting, scourging, and mortification of the flesh brightened the eyes of the spirit and became wonderfully wise. History does not sustain the belief. We read of a Cistercian nun, Passidea of Siena, who would flog herself until she bled and then rub salt and vinegar into the wounds. She found delight in rolling naked in thorn-bushes or on hard stone floors. Once, it is said, she got herself suspended by the feet in a wide chimney over a smoky fire. We trust her reward is great in an invisible world, and doubtless she enjoyed fame while she lived, but you will seek her name in vain today even in Catholic biographical dictionaries and encyclopedias. Elizabeth of Gerton is another lady who is noted in the ancient books as addicted to flogging herself without a bathing costume, but what or where Gerton and Elizabeth were I have been unable to discover.

It will occur to the reader from all this that there was some sort of feminist movement in the 15th and 16th centuries. One must not ascribe this to the new study of the Bible and the spread of Protestant ideas, for Luther and the Reformers generally were confirmed by the study of the Bible in their conviction that woman's place is the home—in Luther's case perhaps we might say the bed—and in Protestant countries feminism found no more favor than in Catholic countries. But a certain strain of feminist assertion runs through the whole of later medieval history. The women of the noble and knightly class during what is called the Age of Chivalry were extremely aggressive. They sometimes led troops of the knights to rob and torture pilgrims, fought each other in bloody tournaments. . . . But I must refer to other works of mine for that. These women neither needed sexual stimulation nor would have scrupled to roast the fat of any monk who urged them to flagellate themselves. When this phase ended in the 15th Century there were two new influences counteracting the Christian subjection of women. One was the example of the dying Arab civilization in Spain in which women had been free and often distinguished. The other was the rebirth of classical literature, showing how during the last four centuries of the Roman Empire women had been free and practically equal to men. But all these influences were anathema to the celibate clergy of the Roman Church, and they guided the ambitions of such gifted or ambitious ladies as remained subject to them along the thorny paths to paradise that I have described. In the Protestant half of Christendom such women found an outlet in politics or social life.

As the law of annual confession to a priest had been passed in the Middle Ages and, logically, the clergy urged folk to confess as often as possible—a woman would go straight to hell if she died in sin before the confession date was due—the clergy got a larger and more intimate power than ever over women and girls as a body. The enormous amount of immorality that ensued must be read in Lea's scholarly and reliable *History of Auricular Confession*. What concerns me here is that the few writers on flagellation all say that at this period, when there was a revival of penitential scourging, the confessors commonly imposed it as a penance and frequently offered their services for the painful task. Popular stories, as I have said, suggest that this was common, and we shall see many instances later. But there was a famous case in Belgium in the 16th Century, thoroughly authenticated because it came into the civil courts and is fully described by the leading Dutch historian of the time, Meteren, with which I may fitly conclude this chapter.

It is the case of Cornelius Adriansen, or, since he was a Franciscan **friar and head of his monastery**, Brother Cornelius. For 30 years Cornelius was the ornament of his order in Bruges, the most eloquent preacher in the town, and a learned theologian and author of theological works. Canon Boileau says that in 1565, when he was noted for the venemence and eloquence of his sermons against heretics, he got together "a number of servants and women who, on the pretext of religion and under oath of loyalty and obedience, were so devoted to him that he not only beat them with knotted cords but made them strip and flogged them on their thighs and arses with rods of willow or birch." Bayle adds in his Dictionary that the man was exiled for a few years from Bruges, but he triumphed over his wicked calumniators—in other words, the ladies succeeded in getting him back—and he continued to illumine the city for a further 20 years.

The valuable notes to later editions of Bayle throw more light on this curious story of what was widely known at the time as "the Gynopygica or Cornelian Discipline." I must leave the reader to guess from the story what the Greek word gynopygica means. Meteren, the Dutch historian, gives the affair considerable length in his *History of the Netherlands.*" Brother Cernelius preached with such feeling against sins of the flesh that ladies who were burdened with a consciousness of them sought him as a confessor. He told many of them (apparently the younger and more comely) that special remedies were required for this sin, but since his action was likely to be misrepresented by evil men they must take an oath of secrecy. Next door to his monastery lived a poor seamstress, and he hired a room in her house, and penitents—maids, matrons, and widows—came there for his special remedy. He made them strip, and he beat them (but gently) on the parts mentioned by Canon Boileau. This went on for 10 years when Brother Cornelius drew into the circle a beautiful 16-year-old girl, daughter of a rich widow who greatly admired him. Girl members of the secret society had told her about it, and she began to confess her sins to Cornelius. After weeks of preparation he persuaded her to visit the house. She refused to strip and was at first impervious to argument. If, said Cornelius, you entrust your soul to me, why not your mere body. At last she stripped but fell in a faint. No other girls were there next time to encourage her by their example. . . . In short, she was soon a regular member of the circle. Like the others she was invited to Brother Cornelius's well-laden table, and he danced with them.

I read between the lines that a blonde had been displaced by the new arrival and there was talk. She ceased to attend, and Cornelius tried to counteract her talk by excommunicating her and another girl who had transferred her tender allegiance to a monk of a rival order. The girl denounced his practices to the Augustinian monks (who, as usual, hated the friars) and presently there was a public scandal and the civil magistrates took up the matter and summoned her. So many girls and women of good family were involved that they attempted to cover it up again, but the facts were widely discussed and they were forced to go on. A terrific scandal ensued. Cornelius was banished, and certain other Franciscan friars whom he had publicly defended were burned for sodomy. And after a few years of impatient exile Cornelius was allowed to return to Bruges, where he died 20 years later in an odor almost of sanctity.

One of the notes which the editor of Bayle adds to the narrative is a quotation from Henri Estienne, a notable French scholar in the first half of the 17th Century and a writer of unusual sobriety. He tells of a father confessor who used to make his penitents exhibit to him the organs with which they had committed the sins they confessed. His bishop took up the matter, and the priest made a spirited defense of his practice. A bodily physician demanded such exhibition and the priest, being a physician of the soul, had at least equal right. He even appealed to the New Testament in which Christ, after working a miracle, said—"Go, show thyself to the priest."

There is some evidence that he was not the only confessor who abused the text. When in the 11th and 12th centuries the Church had imposed celibacy upon the clergy and then found that there was a rapid growth of priests' servants, sisters, cousins, etc., it had been enacted that there was to be no woman under 40 in a priest's house. Many then had two servants and submitted that their combined ages did reach 40. But the full story of all these evasions and hypocrisies would fill a large volume. The spurts of piety, the new outbreaks of self-flagellation, were dying down. The Catholic world was recovering from the panic and resuming its gaiety. But in connection with the 16th Century we have still to consider the rise of the Society of Jesus and the part that the Jesuits played in encouraging flagellation and then in encouraging hypocrisy.

CHAPTER X. THE JESUITS ENCOURAGE WHIPPING—IN OTHERS

In many of these cases of new sisterhoods that we have seen we have noticed the hand of the Jesuit. By an arrangement that seems to have been congenial to both parties the Church maintained its masculine monopoly of power by graciously conceding that the new female saints might have visions and receive direct commands from heaven but each must have a clerical "spiritual director" who would distinguish the genuine from the spurious vision. Protestantism, in allowing the clergy to marry and more or less redeeming sex from the (theoretical) opprobrium of the Church could not have this advantage. In glorifying the Old Testament, about which folk in the Middle Ages had known little and cared less, the Reformers had, it is true, rather increased the subjection of women, but they had at the same time generally contracted the appreciation of sense and sex. Luther landed in a sea of contradictions which makes his character seem enigmatic. The sincerity of his Christian faith is unquestionable yet modern Catholic apologists can extract from his writings a series of sayings that horrify their readers. Much of what the Jesuit writers on him say is sheer libel—as that he kept a harem of ex-nuns and loose women and contracted syphilis—but his language was (especially in his Table Talk) often gross. He quite commonly, for instance, used a four letter word for women that one does not print nowadays. However, in insisting that sex was a normal part of God's creation, provided it was kept within the bounds of marriage—he was willing to allow polygamy when necessary—he abolished for one half the world the tradition of expiating sins by flagellation.

The Catholic reaction, when decades of heavy losses of subscribers forced the authorities at last to listen to the minority of strict prelates and cardinals, was in part to lay a new emphasis on the sense of sin and the virtue of flagellation. Hence the various reforms and new orders of congregations. These, of course, drew off only one in hundreds of the faithful, and it was mainly left to the Jesuits to promote the practice in the world of the laity. Many of the monastic bodies had female branches or Third Orders (or nuns) but the Jesuits, who cultivated women more assiduously than any other body of the clergy or monks, never had one. This surprises no one who knows the history and the character of the Society. The common feeling that intrigue, secrecy, hypocrisy, and a certain unscrupulousness in regard to the means to attain their ends—which are mainly wealth and power—are characteristics of the body is historically correct. Ignatius wanted to found a new order at, as I said, a time when there was a strong conviction in high places in the Church that this community-life under vows always led to hypocrisy and corruption, and he had to use a great deal of intrigue and not a little hypocrisy to get permission to found what, with mock modesty, he called a Society. In particular his early followers were ostentatiously to serve the poor but quietly work to win as many rich and powerful folk, especially ladies and court folk, as possible. The principle that the end justifies the means, which, of course, Jesuits never openly professed in just those terms, was stamped upon the body by its founder from the start.

The main purpose was settled by the history of the time. It was by hook or crook to check the spread of Protestantism and then work for its extirpation. One of the lines taken up for this purpose was the foundation of schools for the sons of the rich and powerful, so the legend that the Jesuits were "great educators" began. In point of fact the hundreds of schools and colleges they established were poisonous establishments for inoculating the children of the rich with sectarian hatred and feeding it by libels of heretics and lies about the Church. Many of their most distinctive methods (lying, tale-bearing, etc.) were contemptible from the educational point of view. We shall see a little more about this in the next chapter but it is part of their crude educational ideal that they insisted everywhere on the merciless flogging of offenders. They did much to prolong the life of that ancient and barbarous practice in the schools of the world.

In regard to adults they strongly encouraged flagellating sisterhoods and lay confraternities wherever this seemed to promote their power of that of the Church. Ignatius of Loyola was not one of the great self-scourgers and his Society did not produce any great flagellant (though some ascetics) like the older orders. In other words, the Jesuits did not really believe, like the older orders in their primitive purity, in self-scourging but were ready at any time to encourage it in others if it suited their aims. A notorious example of their policy in connection with our subject is their "spiritual direction" of that freak of the French monarchy Henry III.

The famous Florentine house of the Medici which figures so prominently in the history of Renaissance Italy, had in the years of its decay given the French a queen, Catherine de Medici; a fat, neurotic woman who combined a slavish devotion to the Church with some strange practices. Her sons were a sickly brood, and acting for the second of them she bitterly persecuted the Huguenots (Protestants) and engineered the horrible St. Bartholomew Massacre. The third son was elected King of Poland, where he shuddered for a few years, but when his brother died he fled by night back to France, "taking with him the crown diamonds and leaving behind the Jesuits," as Michelet says. In spite of the massacre of the Huguenot leaders he found Protestantism still strong, and in a new civil war they forced better terms from him. France was much nearer than is generally supposed to going over to Protestantism in the 16th Century. However, what concerns us here is that Henry III proved to be a morbid and worthless prince who was a notorious sodomist yet the greatest promoter of penitential self-flagellation in that country; and the Jesuits guided his erratic footsteps and were in the closest cooperation with his Medici mother.

From the beginning of his reign Henry had joined the Flagellants. The revival in Italy under Charles Borromeo, to which I have referred, had echoes in the south of France, Toulouse having White, Black, and Blue Penitents while Henry was still in Poland. The movement spread to the old papal city of Avignon, and there Henry and his mother were captivated by the circus processions. Henry joined the Whites—it is said that he prevented his viperish old mother from doing the same— and all three brotherhoods were set up in Paris. Catherine patronized the Blacks and the Cardinal d'Armagnan the Blues, while the great Cardinal de Lorraine carried the crucifix at the head of the scourgers. It is suggested that there was policy in Henry's conduct or in the Jesuit direction of it. Opposed to him were not only the powerful Huguenot party headed by the King of Navarre but the Catholic League which claimed the crown for its candidate. It is thought that Henry chiefly sought to attract the clergy to him by this extraordinary show of piety as he marched in procession through the streets in the common white linen robe of a penitent and laid his scourge vigorously upon his own shoulders. But he was a neurasthenic, and the general opinion of historians is that during these years he oscillated between spasms of morbid piety and debauch.

Paris, in any case, was for the most part greatly amused, for he had with him in the procession two young men whom he had raised to a peerage and loaded with wealth and honors for no visible reason. Everybody spoke of them as his *mignons* or his associates in his perverse practices. The ladies of the court hated him as he, naturally, was no lover of women, and it is said that they wormed his political secrets out his favorites and passed them on to his enemies. The Duchess de Montpensier used to show his friends the scissors she was going to use when they deposed him and made him a monk. He wanted to marry his two sisters to his *mignons*. One fled to a nunnery, and on the marriage of the other he spent several million dollars. The treasury was nearly empty yet he poured money like water upon his ignoble favorites.

It was in these circumstances that the last great processions—not the last appearance but the last large-scale performance—of the Flagellants occurred in Europe. His brotherhood—sisters were excluded—of penitents, whom a friar preacher denounced from the pulpit in Paris as "a fraternity of hypocrites and atheists," had as its patron the Virgin of the Annunciation, and, on that festival of the Virgin, Henry staged a great procession through the streets to the cathedral. The Papal Legate, who must have been quite familiar with the King's perverse practices, gave it his support. Cardinal Birague, Chancellor of the Kingdom, and other great nobles walked in it. Cardinal de Guise, of the second greatest house in France, carried the cross. The Duke of Mayence, of royal blood, was Master of Ceremonies. . . . But what caught the eye of all Paris was the spectacle of the royal profligate and his two ducal *mignons*, dressed in white linen cross-marked robes to the ankles, their whips hanging at their girdles marching and chanting at the head of the long file of "penitents." It rained all day, and in one of the merry caustic songs in which Paris was accustomed to express its feelings in those days was a vivid picture of "the king in a wet sack" and his repentant favorites.

A fortnight later they had another great procession. All through the night they trod the (unpaved and undrained) streets of Paris, blazing candles in their left hands and scourges, which they used occasionally, in the right. The Jesuits encouraged, and the fraternities appeared in many towns. Once or twice Henry and his penitents walked in their linen robes from Paris to Chartres. The king brought a colony of Feuillants, the reform of the Cistercian monks and great flagellators, to Paris and gave them a convent. He had rooms reserved for pious retreat in this and other convents, but the mockers, who were the majority, put a different interpretation on his occasional retirements with a few favorites to these convents.

It all availed nothing from the political angle. The League beat Henry and he fled from Paris. He had the Duke of Guise and his brother, the cross-bearing cardinal, murdered, as a less painful way of securing his crown, and this led to a revolt of Catholic followers. In short, the devotee of the two virgins, Venus and Mary, fled to the camp of the Protestant King of Navarre, a robust lover of women who must have despised him, and he was murdered by a monk. His mother died miserably a month later. And the genial Henry of Navarre concluded, in the historic words, that "Paris was worth a mass," declared himself a Catholic, and suppressed all the fraternities and circus parades.

But it took more than that to dismay the Jesuits. Henry III had had Father Auger, one of the leading French Jesuits, as his spiritual director. But other Jesuits were in the camp of the League stirring the country against him and at first against the Protestant Henry. One Jesuit hailed the murder of the King as "the eternal glory of France." Their chief superior at Paris called from his pulpit for "a second Ehud," to remove Henry of Navarre. They published a work proving that the murder of Kings in the interest of the Church was no sin. And when Rome showed itself a bit nervous about this sudden and profitable conversion of Henry of Navarre, it was above all the Jesuits who smoothed the way for him. The Paris Parlemant expelled them as unscrupulous intriguers for wealth and power but within 10 years they were again round the French throne.

It need hardly be said that they had not a monopoly of such intrigue for the amazing adventures into which it led them—they would rival a modern secret-service novel—excited the jealousy of the other orders. A story of 16th Century monastic life may be quoted in this connection. The theory of the Immaculate Conception was, as I have said, still just a theological opinion and fiercely contested, especially in the great fight of the Franciscan friars, who demanded it, and the Dominican friars, who rejected it. In the city of Bern the Franciscans were making so much progress that their pious opponents concerted a plot. A friar got up as the devil entered the cell of a half-witted brother, Jetzer, howling and breathing fire. He told the brother that he was the spirit of an apostate Dominican who had recently died and he could get release from purgatory only if Brother Jetzel humbly accepted the flagellation from the community, which he did. In short, all this led up to the friar dressing up as the Virgin Mary and telling the half-wit that she was not immaculate. As the fame of these events had gone abroad this, when told, would be a crushing blow to the rival friars. But the performance was too crude, and Jetzer saw that it was all trickery and wanted to expose it. They attempted five times to poison him but he escaped and denounced them, and four friars, Cooper says, were condemned by the civic authorities and executed.

These domestic happenings in rival orders were, however, crude in comparison with the colorful romances (often in fantastic disguises) of the Jesuits. I am concerned here only with their revival of flagellation. They not only insisted on heavy whipping in the schools but whipped lady penitents and natives on the missions. One who worked in Africa severely flogged a native for reverting to idolatry, and the man's women-folk took the revenge of locating their bathing place opposite his windows. It was at all events assumed that he was pained. They followed the Spaniards and Portuguese to South America, and in the profitable agricultural and industrial communities they established—of which a monstrously inaccurate version is circulated by our modern Jesuits—they used the whip freely to wring more work out of the natives. In some places in Europe they got into difficulties with the civic authorities by their fondness for whipping young lady penitents but on this side it will be enough to quote the classic and perfectly authenticated story of the Jesuit Girard and Catherine Cadiere.

Catherine was a devout Catholic lady of 25, with two priest brothers, at Toulon in the early part of the 18th Century when she met the Jesuit. He was renowned as a preacher and therefore as always happened, much sought by young ladies as a confessor. His penitents formed a select and virtuous society under his direction and, subtly and gradually, he induced them to accept flagellation, which he would himself administer. The most active lady of the group gave him great assistance in educating the others, and there does not seem to be much room to doubt that she was his mistress. But his eye fell upon the comely and refined Catherine, and he started a long campaign to get her to accept him as her confessor. The most intimate conversation was now perfectly legitimate. Since I was myself trained for this work the reader may take my word that the priest-confessor not only may but must put extremely delicate questions to a penitent. He cannot permit a girl just to say that she has been unchaste or immodest. He must know not only the particular class of impropriety of which she has been guilty but how far it has gone, and so on. Girard flattered her also by assuring her that she had the gifts of a mystic and visionary, and after a time she confessed a more tender sentiment for him. That is all right, he assured her: "I am united with you in the Sacred Heart of Jesus"! She began, strangely, to have such wicked dreams that she was sure that she was possessed by the devil, and Father Girard undertook to expel the fiend if she would submit wholly to him and agree that more drastic measures were now necessary.

He began to visit her in her home and administer the Cornelian Discipline. He came when she was ill in bed, and she began, she said later, to be concerned about his handling of her. He exacted strict secrecy and, apparently, went the limit. We are told he gave her drugs and then got her taken in at a convent. The nuns regarded his visits with suspicion and enclosed her more strictly in a cell with a small window but, as Cooper puts it, "she used to stretch her body out of the opening and receive the discipline." Voltaire says: "The pretty lady saw God, and Girard saw the pretty lady. Girard had the best of it."

But it seems to me plain that by this time she was as willing as he. The Jesuit, however, tired of her or found a younger penitent and urged her to take the veil. The story runs that the bishop refused to allow her to do this and appointed a new confessor to hear her sins and wicked thoughts. The whole affair now became public, and the Jesuits anticipated danger by holding an inquiry in which they found, of course, that the innocent preacher had been the victim of the wiles of a wicked woman. When the civil authorities then took up the inquiry the Jesuits pulled every string that could be reached and, it is said, not in the least incredibly, spent more than a million francs in bribes. Catherine was incarcerated in a dingy and filthy cell, and every kind of pressure was brought to bear on her to make her retract. But she reached a higher court and, although the judges disagreed, the people of Toulon stoned the Jesuit in the streets. He died shortly afterwards and Catherine disappeared; and, rumor said, the Jesuits alone knew what had become of her.

In several countries Jesuits were similarly brought to justice in connection with women penitents whom they flagellated—one is said to have paid a surgeon to emasculate him so that he could plead incapacity—but not many years after the Girard affair the Jesuits were expelled from France, then from Spain and Portugal, and in 1773 the Society scattered over Europe, generally despised, and employed and honorably treated only by the skeptical monarchs Frederic the Great and Catherine of Russia. In both countries the lash was greatly esteemed so that their fondness for it did not discredit them. But they returned, like so many other medieval evils, after the fall of Napoleon and flagellating fraternities also reappeared, especially in Spain, Portugal, and Latin America.

Apart from an apparently sincere body of Flagellants that was suppressed in Portugal in 1820 the practice now degenerated in most places into a disgusting or ridiculous spectacle. Men joined in the ranks of the occasional flagellating processions often to win the favor of their mistresses, scourging themselves with particular zeal when the procession passed the balcony from which the lady-love watched it, wearing her favorite ribbon on their whip as one the knights had had what is politely called the "favors" (frequently her shift) of their mistresses on their lances in their brutal tournaments. With the steady growth of Liberalism and Socialism in these Latin countries even Catholics began to fight shy of the performance. Where it is still carried out in what is called Holy Week it is as professional as the wearing of swords by officers. At Seville, for instance, where, at least until the civil war, the ancient Holy Week ceremonies were maintained, and I suppose still are, because they are part of the spring attractions for tourists and bring much money to the tradesfolk, the self-flagellting penitents in the mockery of a procession are hired performers, usually men of no character and often criminals. This is the last pitiful phase of the monstrous aberration of piety that filled Europe from the days of Cardinal Damiani.

CHAPTER XI. PENAL FLAGELLATION

In a sense all flagellation except the erotic falls in the category of penal or is a punishment for offenses. In a stricter sense penal flogging is that which is inflicted upon a criminal by the social body which he has outraged by his crime or to deter others from such offenses, by schoolmasters on offending pupils, or by ordinary individuals on servants, wives, and children. But the idea of self-flagellation for sin, particularly when it is imposed or urged by priests who profess to represent the divinity on earth, does not differ in principle. God is conceived as an oriental monarch who is angry and about to punish a man for transgressing his commands, and it is understood that his wrath can be averted if the man punishes himself. We are still in the age of appeasement, but a time will presently come when the historian will invite the psychologist to help him to understand how all those "great men" of whom the modern Catholic apologist boasts can have agreed that God, as an educated person conceived him, could regard with complacency the monk cutting his back to ribbons or the thousands of Flagellants scourging themselves until they bled.

The truth is, of course that "man made God to his own image and likeness," and, just as the Churches still preserve after a hundred transformations of the idea, primitive man's belief that his shadow was a different reality from his body and might survive it, so they maintain the prehistoric principle that a chief or king has a perfect moral right to be angry and to punish. For the latter idea we may say at least that it was a reasonable and inevitable conception in primitive society. In the last century there were still jurists who spoke about the right of society to avenge itself for the affront to its laws or to punish violators of them. Primitive society was nearer to our modern conception. The laws were, except where superstition adulterated them, rules of social conduct, and the aggressor was punished because that seemed to be the only way to secure general observance of the laws. The alliance of morality with religion, which was not original, brought in the idea that the offended majesty of the God must be vindicated by punishment; and the further alliance of kings and priests extended this idea to the offended majesty of the king.

The notion, which we are now supposed to have outgrown, that crimes and offenses must be "punished" was thus lodged essentially in the fabric of civilization, and flagellation was one of the readiest forms of punishment. In the maturity of civilization there is always a tendency to modify this. The Hammurabi Code of Babylonia plainly softens the harshness of the older Sumerian law, and the great Stoic jurists, as they are called—they were probably just as much Epicurean—made great progress in humanizing law. It is obvious that the new religion, representing God as inflicting such a monstrous penalty as eternal torment, put a stop to this humanization, and for 1,500 years the penalties and tortures imposed by the laws of Europe were incredibly barbarous. The heaviest flagellation was by no means the most severe of these. Cutting or burning out eyes, boring tongues with a red-hot iron, public castration, the rack, the wheel, etc., were general over Europe during the whole period of full ecclesiastical authority. Such barbarous tortures as the Spanish Boots—contrivances for screwing wood or metal on the feet and lower part of the legs until the bones were broken—and pouring four gallons of water into a prisoner's body were recognized tortures in French law until the 18th Century. Torture of the genital organs was practiced in Spanish jails until 1900—this I know from men who were in those jails—and according to reliable authors has been practiced in Brazilian and Portuguese jails until our time.

We are, therefore, not in the least surprised that flagellation, which sanctioned or recommended by the Church and used in every school if not every home, had a most conspicuous place in every criminal code. The codes of the Middle Ages, even of the later and more artistic centuries, were so barbarous that it is not necessary to speak of flagellations in that phase. But, while there were many improvements such as (in England, Germany, and other countries) the abolition of the death sentence for heresy, flogging continued without any abatement until the 19th Century. Cooper fills nearly half his large book on the history of flagellation with the penal application of it, and mostly in the 16th, 17th, and 18th centuries. To the modern reader it is more interesting to learn of the religious and the erotic practices, but it is important to understand the monstrous extent and severity of penal flogging in modern times, as our historians take that phrase (from 1550 onward).

British law was then, and until 1817, as crude in regard to flagellation as any, and the lash was laid on, generally by the public executioner, for offenses as trivial as the theft of property of the value of one farthing (half an American cent). In every town there whipping posts of one kind or another, commonly in the form of a cross to the arms of which the offender's hands were tied, or stocks or other modern traps or cages. One of the 18th Century poets wrote:

> In London, and within a mile, I ween,
> There are of jails and prisons full eighteen
> And sixty whipping posts and stocks and cages.

It is hardly necessary to explain that London was then little more than a mile in diameter; in fact, the whipping was generally confined to the central part. As the death sentence was imposed for about 30 crimes besides murder one would think that there were not many left for the lash, but whipping through the streets at the tail of a cart or dragging a man or woman—both were stripped to the waist—from one whipping post to another for a flogging, sometimes four or five in a day, was a familiar spectacle. In the records of a small market town in the center of England we find the payment of 6 pence (12 cents, but then worth much more) "for whipping two people who had the smallpox." A gentleman refuses to pay a barber's bill for making a wig on the ground that it does not fit perfectly. The barber resents it and gets a public whipping. A Scottish person of equivocal character is forced upon a reluctant parish and a woman politely chides him. Four small boys throw a stone or two at a man who beats the woman. The boys get the savage public whipping and when some appeal to the bishop to get the decent woman spared he tells them to "claw the itch out of her shoulders." A magistrate to whom another woman makes a reasonable appeal roars at the court officers: "Skelp her weel, skelp her weel." Quaker women of the most decent and refined type are dragged at the tail of carts, half-naked, for their monstrous heresy. The flogging of loose women, who are common as gooseberries, is a public joke. Two of them came before a judge one day claiming damages for injuries sustained in a fearful whipping, but the police produce evidence, true or false, that they had had a lively carouse after the whipping and returned to their gay ways. Brothels were in those days as common as public-houses, and a woman had to misbehave badly in the streets before the police took an interest in her, yet it was a common sight to see one of them flogged through the town at the tail of a cart.

The common charge on which a whipping was ordered was "vagabondage" and in most cases the letter R ("rogue," then meaning hobo) was burned on the shoulder. But the charge covered all sort of offenses, from stealing a turnip to objecting to the loose life of the clergy, so that the floggers—brawny men who were paid 4 to 8 cents a performance—were rarely jobless. The famous Judge Jefferies of the 18th Century, full-bodied sadistic man of whom the king himself said that he was "more impudent than 10 street-walkers," flogged from one end of England to the other. He had been a dunce and mercilessly whipped at school, so he professed to know from experience that the lash was a most effective teacher of virtue. He delighted to watch the flogging of women, and in winter would cry "Lay on—warm her shoulders for her." He had men whipped from end to end of London, and repeatedly. It is recorded that the picturesque criminal Titus Oates, who still figures in history, received altogether 1,256 strokes with a si-lash whip. Some, who were sentenced to five to 10 years in prison, had to be brought out annually to be whipped through the town. The whip generally consisted of yard-long lashes, fastened on a wooden handle, of twisted and hardened cord, knotted at the end, and as cruel as steel wire. The first stroke generally drew blood. In time the number of lashes was increased to nine and the instrument was called "the cat o' nine tails." When radicalism spread, late in the 18th Century, and the government had an army of spies listening to conversations thousands of educated skeptics or political rebels felt this lash.

The system was, in fact, one of the chief means of maintaining medieval brutality in a large section of the population, for the crowds of women and children ran to see the show as eagerly as they now run to see a distinguished politician. As late as 1862, English magistrates were empowered to order 12 strokes of a leather strap for boys under the age of 14—a case of a boy of 6 is on record— and up to 36 strokes for boys over 14. Inside the jails the lash was used severely to maintain discipline, and so natural did it seem to the callous prisoners that we read of a procuress of the 18th Century who died in jail leaving sufficient money to provide $50 a year for a special sermon, stipulating only that if she was mentioned nothing must be said to her discredit. The Church accepted the charge. Genteel visitors used to intrigue and bribe to get into the jail to see the prisoners lashed. Even in insane asylums in the Middle Ages the lash was used to drive the devil out of the "possessed" man or woman.

There were, we shall see, many humanist skeptics who protested against this universal barbarism but the Church fully supported it and demanded the lash for offenders against itself. I believe that for certain brutal types of crime "the cat" is still ordered by British judges at the jails, and I remember bishops violently protesting 40 to 50 years ago against the proposal to abolish it altogether. One of the best known of them declared that he was ready to administer it with his own hands: not for brutality to women and children, of course, but for such offenses as keeping disorderly houses or playing mackerel, as the French say, to a prostitute.

In Scotland, which considered itself far superior to England from the religious point of view, the barbarity was, if it is possible, worse. It may be said for the Protestants of that country that they merely took over the custom from the Catholic Middle Ages, when the flagellation of criminals and even of suspects (to extort evidence) was savage. But the Calvinists did not bring a spark of humane sentiment or common social wisdom to bear upon it. The witch period was on, and the scourging of men and women to get evidence against others was as bad as the lashing of slaves in the ancient pagan world which they professed to despise. With the adoption of Calvinism the horrors increased. The least shade or suspicion of heresy incurred a cruel flagellation and while such crimes as sodomy naturally multiplied under the puritans, as Buckle shows in his *History of Civilization*, the zealots expended their zeal to the full on loose women. Quite commonly there were pillories at the church doors, and inside there was a "cutty stool," or stool of repentance, on which an offender sat, isolated from and regarded with horror by the congregation throughout the long service. As in England, grave crimes incurred the capital sentence. In fact, there is a case on record of a tailor being beheaded for marrying his first wife's half-brother's daughter. The Church added considerably to the list of offenses which were punished by flagellation, and the list grew still longer when the English government insisted upon forcing episcopalian Christianity on the Presbyterian Scots.

As British law was observed in the American Colonies it need not be said that in the 17th and 18th centuries flagellation was just as common. The early settlers set up pillories and whipping posts like all the other appanages of English civilization and made the same use of them. Quakers who fled from the intolerant brutality of the motherland were just as mercilessly treated in the land of freedom. The pious Quaker who set up as a preacher became a "vagabond" and was terribly flogged, naked to the waist, even when they were refined ladies. Those who helped them were liable to have their ears cut off or a severe scourging. In the few schools the birch swung as merrily as in England, and in the Puritan states sex offenses were almost wiped out in blood. There was, in fact, far more scourging in America because of the general prevalence of black slavery. When the scarred back of a slave reduced his market value, as this was suspected to be evidence of a bad temper, leather straps and wooden ferules, which hurt as much but did not tear the skin and flesh, were substituted. But the brutality of the Legrees of the southern states is well known and I need not enlarge upon it here.

In France flagellation had not as large a place in the penal code and system as in England, though, as I said, worse tortures were kept in the code until the Revolution. The lash was probably more used in lunatic asylums and houses of correction, and I will tell in the next chapter of the vicious use of it in the schools, especially those of the Jesuit and the Lazarist fathers. In the jails it was used commonly enough for the purpose of discipline, and we have occasional cases of the courts ordering it and the public execution of the sentence as in England. The last woman to receive the degradation in France was "Countess" (fictitious title) de la Motte, who was involved with Cardinal de Rohan and others in the affair of the Diamond Necklace, a famous case of fraud and conspiracy. She was severely flogged, semi-nude, at the tail of a cart. Soon afterwards the Revolution, of which many of our historical and literary writers speak with such delicate revulsion occurred, and at least this barbarous type of flagellation was, like so many practices of the ages of faith swept away in a time of humanitarian indignation.

The barbarism was much the same in all countries of Europe and I need not consider each of them. In Russia the knot was almost a national symbol. We must remember that until 1858 the majority of the people were serfs, which means in effect a slave under a Christian regime, and the law authorized the master to flog serfs as much as he liked. The lash fixed to a wooden handle was usually an eight-foot leather thong—one writer says that it was preferably cut from the skin of an old ass and boiled in vinegar—so sharp at the edges, and often ending in wire or a hook, that the first stroke tore the skin and flesh, yet we read of sentences of 200 or even 300 strokes and of drunken nobles and even noble ladies lashing their serfs with unbridled fury. Even when the serfs were "emancipated"—they found that, in fact, they had to labor long years to earn enough to buy it—this brutal treatment of the poor *moujik* continued, and right down to 1910 the brutal lash was inflicted on youths and girls, in large part university students, for political offenses. The generation of Russians that carried the Bolshevik Revolution in 1919 did not consist of workers who had read about the aristocratic landowners of earlier days but of men and women who had lived in such times. Yet, while some of our writers and preachers still speak of the horrors of that Revolution and warn folk against the Atheism that "let loose the passions of the mob," it was, as I show in my *Life of Stalin,* one of the most bloodless revolutions in history.

In Russia, however, the knout was not reserved for serfs and, in the later period, political offenders. Russia was, as we should expect from its geographical position, the last country in Europe to be civilized. It was converted to Christianity in the 10th Century and it was still uncivilized in the days of Peter the Great. That monarch was himself half-barbaric and although he rendered great service to the country on the material side, it was reserved for the French skeptics whom the German-born and educated Catherine brought to her court to begin the humanization of character and institutions. Unfortunately she fell back into reaction, and the average Russian character remained extremely imperfect—drunken, violent, shifty—until the Bolshevik Revolution. The Church, for which our critics of Soviet Russia have so much tenderness, did next to nothing in its 10 centuries of power. The U.S.S.R. has done wonders in raising the general level of character.

Hence the older Russia provides a large amount of material for a history of flagellation. Men and women of every class were knouted or beaten, particularly under Peter the Great. The nobles in turn beat the officials, men flogging their wives, and so on. Catherine flogged her maids, as many ladies did, with her own hands. Her son used to chase the maids round the palace with a whip. He would enjoy an orgy of drink with them at night and then turn upon them with his whip. Nicholas I, in the 19th Century, was even more brutal in ordering the knout. Noble ladies were dragged from their palaces to the jails and birched, with lifted petticoats, on a man's back. The age of political plots and suspicions had begun, and the Church raged against the multiplication of sects and against subjects of the Roman Pope. Poland was at that time a province of Russia, and the stories told in the Catholic literature of the sufferings of the priests and nuns are substantially true. Cooper has a chapter of horrors on the nuns of Minsk in 1840. Large numbers of them died under the lash and the survivors were put in sacks and for three hours dragged backward and forward across a freezing lake. The Catholic bishop said that he would take three skins off them, "one that they had received from God and two from the Tsar." Catholics who talk about persecution under the Bolsheviks—this was really legal prosecution for proved treason—ought to read the story of this savage Orthodox persecution in their own Catholic Encyclopedia.

The degradation of the Orthodox Church, corresponding to that of the Roman Church in the Middle Ages, led to the appearance of a number of native Russian sects, and in some of these we get the practice of self-flagellation, though in Russia in the old crooked days the saint was never far away from the devil. The Starevests or Old Believers, in the first half of the 19th Century, stripped themselves to the waist and lashed themselves in the good old theological fashion until their backs were torn. It appears that, like the original Flagellants of the Middle Ages, they were genuine ascetics and sound believers in the theory that God loves blood and pain. Other Russian sects, which met in dark corners, were not so edifying. The Khlisti, which means the Scourgers, I believe, mixed sensuality with asceticism in the more morbid religious fashion. Their meetings were orgies at which they had a young girl representing the Virgin whom they raped and sacrificed, but in their wild dance round her, as she sat in a tub of warm water, they lashed themselves vigorously. Some reminiscence of an old fertility cult, which laid stress on sex, was apparently mixed with Christian formulae. Rasputin is said to have belonged to this sect, but he did not adulterate its more joyous features with ascetic practices.

There would be little point in surveying the customs of all countries. China has always been a classic land of beating but the instrument was usually the bamboo, not a lash, so that it hardly comes within our range. The Turks and Arabs, especially the Arab slave-drivers, were familiar with the lash, and, as everybody knows, the Boers of South Africa used a vicious whip, the syjambok (of hippopotamus hide), on the natives mercilessly. All countries in Europe made the same penal use of it as the British, and in the penal colonies like Australia, to which large numbers of English convicts (often decent political radicals) were sent at the beginning of the last century, flagellation of the most brutal type was almost a daily event. It was just as brutal in the navies, especially the British. The sailor of those days was a rough type but the savage whipping tended to confirm him in his animalism. But I need not indulge in moral or philosophical reflections. Far more solid than any argument about codes of conduct is the plain fact that this brutal practice, which makes a trail of blood across the history of civilization, was indignantly repudiated by the human conscience when the ages of faith ended and the age of skepticism began.

CHAPTER XII. FLOGGING IN THE SCHOOL

An attempt was made at one time by French writers to give the name Orbelianism to the practice of flogging school children. The word is taken from the name of an ancient Roman schoolmaster who, Horace tells us, was famous for his fondness for the rod, and it reminds us that the practice goes far back in history. Indeed the biblical "Spare the rod and spoil the child," which was one of the excuses for child-flogging in Christian days, may seem to date the practice much earlier. There seems to have been little schooling amongst the early Hebrews—the above maxim is addressed to parents—but amongst the relics of ancient Egypt we have ample traces both of schools and corporal punishment. "A boy's ears grow on his back" (some translate "backside") is said to have been one of the golden rules of teachers in ancient Egypt. However that may be, the Roman teacher was lavish with the birch, the ferule (leather strap), or the stick, though educationists like Quintilian and novelists like Plutarch opposed the practice.

The history of school-flagellation is almost a blank from the 4th to the 12th Century because, as most of my readers will know, few schools existed in the Dark Age. An historian of education has said that the number of schools in existence at any one time from the middle of the 5th to the middle of the 11th Century could be counted on one's fingers. As these few were generally in monasteries and the pupils were usually novices we may be sure that the lash was familiar enough. When free schools began to spread in the second part of the 11th Century discipline was poor. The famous wandering scholars who migrated from town to town did not so much seek wisdom as amusement and sensation. In such cities as Paris, where there were thousands of them, they were a wild horde fighting, drinking, and indulging in less respectable avocations, particularly needing to be restrained by the King's forces. In time the monks and bishops captured the schools, preparatory schools were established under firm masters, and the rule of the rod in the school began again.

In practically the whole of the fields of flagellation which I covered in the last chapter the men and women were naked to the waist, and the heavy lash fell upon bare backs and shoulders. In practically all boys' schools and colleges and a very large part of the girls' schools it was the lower half of the body that was denuded. As I have previously said, religious writers give their readers a totally false impression of the "modesty" of the ages of belief. Cooper reproduces an illustration from a prayer-book that was used in the cathedral of Chartres in 1526. It represents the castigation of a pupil in school and has on the margin in Latin the words "The beginning of wisdom." The chief thing that confronts the pious lady or girl who reads her prayers from the book in church is the ripe stern of a boy of 13 or 14 who is bending for the lash. He hardly dare so expose himself even in a solitary pool today. Yet this was a common theme of painters and sculptors in the Middle Ages, and the custom of lowering the pants for the sacrifice was continued well into the 19th Century. The instrument of torture used in school was generally the birch—a bunch of thin branches of birch or willow—but sometimes a leather strop or in more recent times, a strip of whalebone or a cane. Many schools had whipping blocks something like execution blocks, over which the kneeling culprit spread himself, but the teacher's knee or the back of another pupil or school attendant generally sufficed.

Schools were, as I said, few in Europe until the 11th Century but with the spread of schools in the 12th and 13th centuries the rod became almost a symbol of school life. Private tutors used it as freely as schoolmasters, and many a well-known monarch had his stern warmed in boyhood and insisted that his sons should receive the same lesson in virtue. In Germany a master was presented with a birch, as a symbol of office, when he was appointed, and in some parts the Church recognized a Feast of the Birch. "O thou, dear birch, make me good so that I fall not into the ways of crime," the pupil was taught to address it. Quite commonly he was compelled to kiss it before or after administration, and men of distinction down to the 19th Century maintained that in their own experience it had proved a valuable part of their education. "My master whipped me well," said the sententious Dr. Johnson, "and without that, sir I should have done nothing." The poet Crabbe quotes saying:

Students, he said, like horses on the road
Must be well lashed before they take the load.

When the controversy arose, we shall see, the rod had defenders, but, from the time when schools, apart from the theological, multiplied in Europe humanists attacked the practice. Erasmus and Montaigne criticized it, and in Protestant England the skeptic Locke said that "the discipline of the whip is a servile discipline and makes servile characters."

Erasmus had little influence in this matter, and his friend, the Christian humanist, Dean Colet, was a great flogger and used to have the boys brought before him after dinner for the purpose. On the continent of Europe the Jesuits, as I said, made matters worse with their zeal for flagellation. A French pamphlet of the year 1764 severely criticized their system. The author says that they usually ordered 60 or 70 strokes of a heavy lash and in some cases 200 or 300; and they so far anticipated modern psychology as to observe that after a number of strokes the victim became more or less numb so they ordered intervals for him to recover the full sense of pain. Their schools were notorious for flogging of both boys and girls with uplifted skirts and often caricatured until the 19th Century when they began to discover the error of their ways. They had, as will be remembered, been suppressed by the Pope, to the general delight of Europe, in the 18th Century and had during the period of suppression been engaged to teach in the schools of Frederic the Great and Catherine of Russia. We need not look for any supernatural scource of their saner ideas in the 19th Century.

In the 17th Century they had rivals in the Lazarist fathers who, though founded for the purpose of teaching the children of the poor in country districts, where the percentage of illiteracy until the Revolution was about 99 and a fraction, soon, like the Jesuits, smelt the wealth of the cities. Their schools at Paris flogged even more zealously than those of the Jesuits. Indeed, they became such recognized experts on the art of communicating lessons of virtue through the lumbar nerves that parents, guardians, tutors, etc., used to pay them small fees to chastise their children or charges for them. There were many misadventures when the boy was sent to the school with the fee and a letter of introduction but doubtless the parents generally examined the boy's tail to see that the order had been carried out. There was presently another religious congregation of teachers, the Brothers of Christian Doctrine, who held to old-fashioned methods until an increasingly wicked and godless world intervened. As early as 1832 a priest was prosecuted and fined in France for whipping a boy.

Many quaint customs developed in different countries in connection with this form of chastisement. In some places in Holland all the boys at the beginning of the vacation had to jump through a hoop, and the master had a swipe at each with a cane as he jumped. In other places they had to pass between his legs to get out of the school and he thrashed them as they bent to do so. The boys were taught to sing a cheerful song about the lash, and there was not the somber atmosphere of the Jesuit school. Cooper says that the girls in their schools had to present a nude surface down to the present century.

In Germany there was a special officer of a school to minister the birch, even to youths of 17 and 18. He wore a long blue cloak and was known to the boys as the Blue Man. Many masters, however, felt that they were entitled to discharge this agreeable function themselves. There is a record of a German schoolmaster who kept tally and at the end of 51 years as the head of a large school proudly announced that he had inflicted 911,500 canings, 121,000 floggings, 200,000 slappings, 126,000 taps with a ruler, and 16,200 boxes on the ears. At Augsburg a school was kept by a body of nuns who were popularly known as the Boot Nuns, because their rule compelled them to wear light boots even in winter. They taught boys from 6 to 10 years of age and their method of punishment was to lower the pants and make the boy stick his head into an empty stove to get the correct posture. In some schools there was a window to the whipping room through which Jesuit priests used to watch the course of the proceedings.

English schools were until the 19th Century second to none in the art of flogging, and in no other country was there a fiercer fight over the issue, "To Flog or not to Flog." Diaries and volumes of reminiscences are full of picturesque anecdotes about it in "the good old days." One is told of a charity school for girls in the 18th Century and the more or less aristocratic ladies who ran it. It was housed in a noble old mansion and for the age almost luxurious. A wicked earl in London had built it in the country for his mistress, as every child knew, since his coronet was proudly embroidered on their gloves. One of the ladies, dark, thin, and vinegary, liked to give floggings herself and would lay on until she was exhausted. The great event of each dull day was the whipping hour, from 4 to 5 every afternoon. The father and good-natured dame sat looking on while her sister worked, or brought her maid, a willing collaborator to wield the whalebone rod for her; for a French lady had pointed out that the whalebone rod hurt quite as much and did not tear the skin. If the ladies had visitors they brought them to the school to see the performance. The girl offender would strip and fold her clothes neatly, then kneel and kiss the rod in the French manner. The girl was then taken across her back by a robust servant and the appropriate part was soundly flogged.

Another description is of an aristocratic girls' school about the beginning of the 19th Century. The offender would approach the desk of the governess and politely ask permission to bring the birch. She brought it on a cushion and presented it on her knees, and she got it on her arms and shoulders if the offense were trivial. For a grave offense such as stealing the rod had to be applied more closely and lower down before the whole school. Girls of 16 and 17 were clad in a sort of nightdress and sometimes beaten until they bled, their feet being fastened in some contrivance to keep them still. In other accounts of schools for such young ladies in the 18th Century it is expressly said that the birch was administered on the bare buttocks. There was a letter in the London press from an Irishman who said that his niece had been so treated and he had given the mistress a dose of her own medicine. But until recent times few parents protested. As late as 1870 ladies advertised for schools at which a difficult girl would get the birch, and at a finishing school for young ladies of 14 to 17 in Havana the birch was still laid upon a nude surface in 1836.

In what are called the "public schools" (Eton, Harrow, etc.) for the sons of the rich—until recent years they would have sternly excluded sons of the general public even if the father could find the high cost—whipping was as normal a part of the routine as the daily Church of England service. A story used to be told of a distinguished man who, meeting the master of his old school, observed that they had often met before. "I don't remember your face, sir," said the master. "No," said the man, "I fear you were more familiar with my other end." A variation of the story is that when a man reminded a retired master that he had often flogged him, the master said: "I don't remember—boys' rears are·very much the same." It is related of the painter Vandyk that once at school he painted a portrait of the master on the stern of a boy who was to be whipped. The master roared with laughter when the pants came down and let off the culprit.

Masters differed greatly. Some, whether from a sadistic streak or no, beat the boys ferociously. At the Merchant Taylors (public) School in London one of these made such an impression on the boys that they clandestinely published a periodical which they called "The Flagellant." The editor, who was detected and expelled, was the poet Southey. Other masters were jovial about it. One of these had a boy unbreeched before him one day while a group stood by waiting their turn. The master turned to the boys and said: "I ask the banns of matrimony between this boy's buttocks and Lady Birch, if any of those here present knows of any impediment let him speak." One of the boys raised his hand and said: "I forbid the banns, sir." When he was asked on what grounds he said: "Because the parties are not agreed, sir."

At Winchester School it was the ancient tradition for centuries that the birch should be made of apple-tree twigs fitted into a wooden handle. At Shrewsbury School the flogging took place in a room without any windows, but in most places the rod was given before the other boys and often before visitors to the school. It was one of the recreations of many of the idle rich of the time to get permission to see a flogging either in the school, the barracks, or jail. We must remember that only a hundred years ago life was still brutal both in Britain and America. No gloves were used in fights and there were few rules, yet crowds went to them as they do today. A fight was so popular that in the first quarter at least of the last century hundreds occurred daily in every class. There were prize fights of women and of scholars—in one famous case to the death. Folk who objected were sissies. Fighting "hardened" youth, and commonly enough educated men agreed that it taught self-control. In towns where the big schools were situated "town and gown" fights—scholars and townsfolk—of the most violent character were frequent. Animal fights of a dozen types—dogs, rats, cocks, bears, etc.— were highly esteemed. Paddling on the buttocks was a small matter in such a world.

In many cases, as many will have learned from the Hollywood film, "A Yank at Eton," the older boys were empowered to chastise the fleshy parts of the younger boys for slight offenses. The essayist Charles Lamb tells us that he was frequently summoned from bed to get the strop from such a monitor. Some of these used, when there was a disturbance in the dormitory at night, to drag the boys out of the six beds that happened to be nearest the door and give collective chastisement. I think it is Lamb who tells the story of a pupil who when he became a man of distinction and prosperity, went to the town where his school had been and invited to dinner a master who had given him many a drastic birching. When the master, who was greatly flattered, came he was ordered to strip for a good thrashing. He persuaded his host that they ought to dine first and he got him into so mellow a condition that the flogging was forgotten. When nudity of the relevant part began to be pushed out of the fashion the boys, naturally, put padding, preferably of leather, which made no noise, in the seats of their pants. One Scottish master who preferred the flat of his hand on the nude stern noticed that the musical note differed in different boys so when he had a dozen to chastize he arranged them in a series and invited other masters to come and "hear me play my organ."

There were schools where parents were charged for the castigation of their boys. At Eton School, where flogging was so normal a part of life that it was customary for a new schoolmaster to be presented by the Captain of the school with an elegant birch, tied with blue ribbon, on his arrival, the account sent to parents always included $5 for flogging whether a boy had had to be punished or not. It was said that a junior master once wrote the names of the boys who were to be confirmed on the form which was used for boys to be flogged. The mistake was explained in time to the headmaster but he refused to give up his right to flog them. A case is on record of a headmaster having a list of 80 culprits at the close of the day. He cleared off the lot after dinner.

Though schoolmasters never went so far as those brothel mistresses in China who used to put cats in the seat of the loose pants of the young ladies before they played on them, the humanitarian sentiment that spread, chiefly from the works of the French skeptics, in the second half of the 18th Century, brought out many protests against the practice. There was almost as heated a discussion in England as there is today about the atom-bomb. We still have a long, breezy defense of the rod, a poem titled *The Rodeads*, that was published early in the 19th Century by one of the best known dramatists of the time, George Colman (junior). He imagines a master saying:

> But now for years my chief delight has been
> To scourge the obnoxious stripling of sixteen,
> Horsed at nice angle on the sturdy back
> Of one whose faithful aid I never lack.

On rainy days, especially, using the rod lifts his depression, he says. Even the servants down below cheer themselves by whipping the kitchen boy. They "punish his buttocks for their own disgrace" and "the housemaids whip him their hot lust to slake." The schoolmaster deserves the reward of using the cane or birch when he has done a hard day's work. There ought to be Whipping Clubs to which young children could be sent for chastisement, and amateurs might pay for the pleasure of laying the birch on them.

> The clergy, careless of the word of God,
> Too often spoil the child and spare the rod.

And he ends in a sort of ecstasy:

> Delightful sport, whose never-failing charm
> Makes young blood tingle and makes old blood warm.

England was then lapsing into the new phase of brutality brought upon it by the long Napoleonic war and the excuse which the French Revolution gave for the vile treatment of rebels against Church and state. Flogging in the schools continued, and in the jails, army, and navy, and penal colonies was worse than ever. But humanitarian radicalism raised its bloody head again when the reaction after Waterloo began to wear off. In regard to flagellation it was aided by the new puritanical sentiment that spread in Europe, especially in Victorian England. Flogging the bare flesh, especially in the case of girls, soon had to cease. There were successful prosecutions of masters of workhouse schools who put girls of 13 and 14 over their knees. Even in the case of boys the anti-floggers not only argued that there was indecent exposure but delicately intimated a fact which most folk know, that there was a strong suspicion of the horrid taint of lust in the floggers. In modern terminology this practice of birching or strapping the nude buttocks of boys in the early teens promoted the taste for perverse conduct in the flogger and for erotic flagellation in the boy. We return to that point in the last chapter.

When the practice of stripping disappeared the growing sentiment of the 19th Century struck at the whole principle of the rod. Reformist pedagogists denied the supposed educational value of flogging; and they were in line with the strong and increasingly successful demand for penal reform. The plain truth was that conduct was improving all round, in the school, the army, and the general life of the city, in proportion as the old brutality was abolished. Schoolmasters had to take refuge in the familiar compromise of caning pupils on the hands. It was a universal practice when I entered upon school-life soon after 1870. I am assuming that this development was much the same in America as in Europe, but no writer has collected the material in the case of the American schools and it hardly seems necessary. There was a world movement away from medieval barbarism.

Toward the end of the century there was a broad and strong agitation against all corporal punishment. Masters who still (generally in a fit of temper) laid the cane upon the backs and shoulders of pupils, even over their clothing, were apt to be prosecuted for assault by parents. The battle is practically over and it would be hard to find a master today who does not recognize that general conduct is better than ever in schools and the atmosphere more wholesome. The whole story makes the recent plea that we want more religion in schools ironic. This gross tradition was never censured by the Church during its 13 or 14 centuries of despotic power and supposed moral guidance, and the modern reformers who fought for sanity and decency in the 19th Century got little assistance from the ecclesiastical side.

CHAPTER XIII. DOMESTIC FLAGELLATION

.... The third and by no means least form of this penal or punishment flagellation, which was one of the grossest aberrations of the days when an arbitrary command instead of social interest was made the basis of the moral sense, was flogging in the home or the social life. Since the universe was run by an arbitrary ruler, and one who set so fearful an example of the punishment of offenders, each person in authority in some sphere or other followed the august lead. The father whipped his wife and children, the master or mistress had unrestricted power to chastise the servants, the craftsman beat the apprentices, the employer savagely beat such junior employes as (by law) could not transfer to another master, and so on; and, naturally, in such a world of flagellation citizens were easily provoked to fall upon each other. Thomas Carlyle describes in one of his letters how as late as 1840 he saw the British employers truculently beat the children (from 8 or 9 upward) whom the benevolent government lent them instead of having to keep them—they were mostly unwanted bastards—in the workhouses. The underfed youngsters, housed at night in kennels or barns or (at the best) boiler-houses, were beaten with leather belts, sometimes iron chains, when they had worked 10 or more hours in a fetid mill and began to drop. This was done all over Britain, and in many industrial parts of America, as late as 100 years ago. And it was no consequence of the Industrial Revolution but near the last chapter of a story of flagellation of the weak that stretched more than 1,000 years back into history.

What was said in the early chapters of this work will remind the reader that this was not, like the persecution of heresy, an evil introduced into Europe by the Christian system. It was inherited from the ancient world. Although woman in Egypt and Babylonia had been free and independent and therefore not likely to have suffered much from masculine brutality—she had liberal rights of divorce—the new civilization was based upon two codes of law that recognized the autocracy of the male parent and an extensive practice of slavery: the Roman and the Hebrew codes. How far the Stoic-Epicurean reform of Roman ideas and customs had proceeded by the 4th Century we cannot precisely say, but I have a good knowledge of the literature of that century and it affords little evidence of cruelty to wives, children, slaves, or servants. The schoolmasters, it is true, still brandished the rod, but, as I said, schools almost ceased to exist when the Roman Empire fell, and when they multiplied in the later Middle Ages the lash was so familiar that teachers had no need to learn from classic literature to apply it mildly, though more intimately, to the less vulnerable parts of their pupils.

The Old Testament was much more responsible for the destruction of the freedom and almost equality which woman had won in later Roman days. Only a week or two ago I saw, passing the uncurtained window of the dining room of a house on some festival, how father and son feasted at table while mother and daughter waited on them. To my knowledge that man, who was not at all religious, occasionally beat his wife and daughter.

It is only recently, and in special synagogues, that women have been put on a footing with the men even in the religious service. From their sacred book and their own dreary puritanism the Fathers of the Church deduced painfully contemptuous sentiments about women. These were almost lost in the sight of dense ignorance that fell upon Europe after the 5th Century, when not one in a hundred even of the clerical minority who were more or less literate ever read the Fathers. But, as we saw, the ascetic movement which prevailed in the Church just when, in the 11th Century, civilization began to creep into it once more, taught the same puritanical contempt of women as well as a morbid esteem of flagellation.

This movement was, however, not only limited in its influence and soon swamped by a looser life than ever but it was counteracted by the troubadour movement. The laws of the Teutonic nations before that time had confirmed the despotism of the husband and father. Anglo-Saxon law, for instance, permitted the husband to beat his wife "severely" with a whip or a stick. Welsh law allowed "three blows with a broomstick on any part of her person except the head." In a later age the law was modified, but both in England and the Eastern States of America, it, until the 19th Century, allowed a husband (without fear of a charge of assault) to beat his "wife with a stick if it was no thicker than his thumb." It said nothing about a lash, and it was, even in my own boyhood in the north of England, usual for the workers to wear heavy leather belts, with brass knuckles, and it was with these that they usually beat their wives. In the '70s I personally knew workingmen who every Saturday night, when they were full to the lips with beer, beat their wives—in some cases meek, sober, inoffensive women—with their belts until they dropped. There is painful evidence that that had been the general lot of wives of the workers since the Dark Age.

As I said, the women of the knightly class in the later Middle Ages were by no means subject to their husbands. The romantic idea that the men now idealized their wives and daughters and would not dream of assaulting them is as absurd as the idea that the early Bolsheviks tried to abolish marriage. The literature of the time (roughly 1100 to 1400), the mass of stories, epics, songs, etc., that remain to us, show that when the man was definitely the stronger or when he met an unprotected maid on the road he used her brutally. But the women as a body were robust and self-assertive and passed with great freedom from one husband or lover to another. All the authoritative histories of the time admit that. An extraordinary number of the "noble" women of the time were sheer gangsters, notorious for torture and murder. But they united with their "noble" husbands in brutality to the "lower orders," who were nine-tenths of the community. Flagellation was too mild an exercise for these viragoes and their men. Mutilation (eyes, ears, noses, testicles, hands, feet, tongues) was more common than the use of the whip.

It is ironic that with the extinction of this class—the ironclad nobles living in impregnable castles and making raids from them were replaced about the end of the Middle Ages by silk-clad courtiers (thanks largely to the introduction of gunpowder)—and their savagery a great age of flagellation arose, as we saw in the preceding two chapters. In America this was confirmed by the heavy use of the whip on the plantations, but it was common enough in the north. The *Gazeteer*, a British publication, had in 1771 an amusing story that illustrates this.

A captain of an English vessel was put in the stocks at Boston for the terrible offense of taking a walk on a Sunday and was drenched with pious exhortations. It would be interesting to know the nautical language with which he replied in his own mind, but he professed that he was converted, and before sailing he invited the city-fathers to dine on his ship. At the close of the meal his sailors stripped the Puritans to the waist on the deck and laid about them with the cat o' nine tails.

The reader will know enough about whipping in America and I will continue to confine my attention to Europe. English literature in every century gives evidence of the 15th Century advising the husband:

> Thou wilt be constrained her head to punch
> And let not thine eye then spare her.
> Grasp the first weapon that comes to hand,

73

Horsewhip or cudgel or walking stick,
Or batter her with the warming pan.

England was particularly demoralized in that century by the long and savage civil war that is known as the Wars of the Roses, and the impulse to violence was encouraged in every class. To those days belongs the cynical popular saying, which always provoked a laugh until the last century:

A woman, an ass, and a walunt-tree,
The more you beat 'em the better they be.

Literature multiplied in the renaissance of the next century but it shows no improvement as regards flogging. The multiplication of schools and insistence of such educationists of fine character as Dean Colet that the birch and strap were a healthy part of education encouraged the feeling. Diaries and anecdote writers and court gossipers speak lightly of whipping in every class. Queen Elizabeth beat maids with her own hand as we should expect that semi-masculine or "third sex" lady to do. Cooper reproduces a long passage from the diary of an aristocratic lady who ingeniously lets us see the frame of mind of women of her class. She flogged her maids almost every day, and after a particularly heavy flagellation of one for allowing the son of the house to flirt with her she wrote in her diary:

The girl's person is plump and firm, and she is a cleanly person such as I have not whipt for a long time.

We suspect a tinge of sadistic feeling and it is clear that the maid was stripped at least to the waist. The lady adds that in the middle of the whipping ceremony in her chamber she heard a loud laugh at the window. Her son had mounted a ladder outside and enjoyed the performance. The father took him in hand and impressed the decalogue upon his more sensitive parts. Pepys Diary, of the next century, often speaks of flagellation, and as placidly as it describes the weather.

Amongst the common people wife-beating was a joke. In some parts of the country the neighbors gathered outside the cottage and provided an orchestral accompaniment on kettles and pans and by blowing horns. There were, of course, robust women who turned upon their husband and beat him. The men did not like such dangerous violations of the masculine prerogative, and in many places they made a demonstration against the husband. They gathered outside the house with horns on their heads—the usual reproach of a cuckold—a chemise on a pole, and drums and other noisy instruments, singing: "Ye round-headed cuckolds, come dig, come dig." Different districts had their variation of the rite, and as late as the 18th Century one of Hogarth's paintings shows the humiliating treatment by neighbors of a man whose wife beat him. Husband and wife are tied back to back on a horse, and the woman belabors him with a frying pan.

Butler, the great satirical poet of the 17th Century, has a passage in *Hudibras* which shows that "gentlefolk" were sometimes as robust as fishwives:

Did not a certain lady whip
Of late, her husband's own lordship,
And, tho' a grandee of the House (of Lords),
Chase him with fundamental blows?
Tied him stark naked to a bed-post
And firked his hide as if she'd rid post,
And after in the Sessions Court,
Where whipping is judged, had honor for it?

Notes to the poem inform us that this referred to an actual incident of the time. Lord Munson, himself a judge, was a trimmer in politics and his wife despised him for continually changing sides in those changeful days. . With the help of her maids she stripped him, tied him to the bed post, and flogged him. He took her to court but the magistrates seem to have been of the political party he had last left and she was honorably acquitted.

But the robust woman was a rare exception. Century by century the flogging of wives and mistresses, especially on suspicion of disloyalty, continued. It was perfectly legal, and the women of the higher class had, as we saw in the last chapter, been thoroughly introduced to the rod at school. Children were flogged almost daily for trivial offenses. In some places there was a custom of flogging all the children of the house periodically on the principle that prevention is better than cure. Maids and serving boys were, of course, constantly flogged. The Puritan authorities of the 17th Century had no objection to the flagellation but they made a law that male servants must be flogged by the master and maids by the mistress. A London clergyman of the 18th Century was taken to court on the charge that he chastised his wife's maid in the ancient manner or upon a denuded surface. The man's mood is plain enough, but in court he vigorously pleaded that he had a religious and legal right to do it.

The range of the lash was extended by the system of apprenticeship that had developed out of the guild system of the Middle Ages. Tradesmen and women (dressmakers, milliners, etc.) had young folk indented as apprentices and living in the house; and the police could be engaged to trace them and bring them back if they ran away. Their condition depended upon the character of the master or mistress but it was as a rule little better than slavery; and we must not forget that there were in the 17th and 18th Century thousands of colored slaves from the West Indies in England. Even mistresses beat their apprentices heavily, and the law gave them no protection; though when, as happened a few times, the apprentices turned upon the mistress and gave her a dose of her medicine the law was outraged. A doggerel of the time giving good advice to girl apprentices warns them to rise promptly in the morning. "Lest quickly your mistress uncover you bare." "I'll thrash you within an inch of your life" was not an idle phrase in those days.

In the second half of the 18th Century, when infidelity spread from France, protests against the orgy of flogging began to be heard. One paper of the gentlefolk published a whole series of letters for and against. A lady recommending a compromise said that they ought to drop "the gross Dutch word flogging" and keep to "the refined English expression "chastisement." Liberalism and radicalism, which always brought humanitarianism with them, really spread widely in England in the second half of the 18th Century, and the defense of flogging was mainly taken up by Tories and Church folk. But the lying stories of French refugees about the Revolution—stories still cherished in sectarian literature—enabled the reactionaries to crush the Liberals and all their new-fangled sentiments. The clergy supported the reactionaries and glibly quoted the advice of a forger of 2,500 years earlier to "spare not the rod." The country became accustomed to the brutal treatment of political rebels, and hope of relief for wives, children, apprentices, soldiers, sailors, etc., dropped.

In 1926 I published a work (*A Century of Stupendous Progress*) for which I made a detailed and laborious study of life in Britain in 1825 and contrasted it with 1925. The brutality of life and the suffering of workers, women, and children were still revolting. In places convicted men were still whipped through the streets of a city while the authorities and citizens smilingly looked on. Gross crime was especially common, and if the offender was a gentleman or a clergyman he was rarely prosecuted or punished. The papers told lightly of brutalities and grossness among the workers. As divorce under the law of the time was possible only for the noble or rich—there had to be a costly Act of Parliament for each divorce, as the Church insisted on making it almost impossible—the domestic consequences can be guessed. Still in 1825 workingmen in provincial towns would put their wives, sometimes with ropes or halters round their necks, at auction on market day and, after uproarious bidding, hand them over for $2 or a gallon of ale. It is not necessary to say that the beating of wives and children went on much the same as in the Middle Ages.

75

The situation was generally as bad in all European countries and I need not describe it at any length. In France flogging was as common as in England but more with the cane than the whip. The idea of religious self-flagellation did not entirely disappear when the Parliament suppressed the societies of Flagellants that Henry III and the Jesuits had established. For a time the practice continued among the more ascetic of the Jesuits, a powerful branch of the Catholics of Paris who, though they gave the Jesuits a feeble excuse to denounce them as doctrinal heretics, were really obnoxious to the authorities because they insisted on austerity of life. When they suppressed the idea of self-flagellation, it was known only in cases of hypocrisy like that of the Jesuit Girard, which I gave in an earlier chapter. The French *Grande Encyclopé*die gives a curious case that occurred in the 18th Century, the case of the brothers Bonjour and their Farcinist Flagellants.

The elder brother was a parish priest who made himself popular by advocating in his sermons that the rich ought to share their advantages with the poor. The landowner and the wealthier parishioners got the bishop to remove him, and in his new charge at the village of Farcinos he made his younger brother the curate. For eight years they won high prestige for the purity of their morals and their charity, and the older man then resigned his position to the younger who, after eloquent protests of his unworthiness took charge and brought another priest to assist him. It is hardly necessary to explain that at this time, the eve of the Revolution or about 1780, a chaste priest was regarded as exceptionally holy, and the three priests, living together, edified the whole district by their virtues. It was only after the exposure that a search of their house was discovered a large quantity of choice foods and wines. One can imagine the neurotic excitement of the women and girls of the district and the next thing was that he had crucified a girl, who had asked him to do so in the chapel and then cured her.

Whether the priests had had a secret group of girls sharing their banquets for some time is not clear but it is on record that a group assisted with the priests at the "crucifixion." However that may be they were presently known to have a company of followers, girls and women, who foregathered with them in a barn by night for flagellation. There was no light and the doors were closed, but the old priest entered by a window and flogged them, nude or half-nude. It was so much to their liking that they began to pester "the Little Papa," as they called him, in the daytime and press him to make them happy. The sect was said to advocate communism, and when the husbands of some of them saw that food disappeared from their homes they denounced the priest to the authorities. The elder brother was banished from the district and the younger put in prison. But he was, of course, "miraculously" liberated and the crucified girl joined him in Paris and recommended the pious imposture. She was said to have had long feasts during which nothing passed her lips but human excrements. A number of the villagers from Farcines joined them and again formed a society of Flagellants, but it was, as I said, the eve of the Revolution, and the wicked revolutionaries scattered the pious group and opened the eyes of the people.

Of the schools it is not necessary to speak as caning and flogging was in every country as normal a part of the routine of school life as singing hymns, but until the Revolution there was a good deal of flagellation, and some self-flagellation, in social and private life. The abbé Granet tells an amusing story of an incident at Paris in the 18th Century. One of the nobles, the Duc de Vegas, reverted to the idea that self-flagellation for his sins was pleasing to the Lord—as well as diverting to the people. About 100 of his friends and servants preceded him with wax candles burning. One day his procession entered a narrow street just when another self-flagellating noble with his retinue entered the street at the other end. Neither would yield and the servants began to daub and belabor each other with the candles. The gentlemen of their suites then fell upon each other with swords, and finally the two nobles fought it out with their lashes.

"Noble" ladies, it appears, often had rivals seized and flogged by their lackeys. The Marchioness de Tresnel had the Dame de Liancourt, of inferior rank but high pretentions, dragged from her coach and flogged. Another noble lady was stung by hearing praise of the beauty of a peasant girl in her district and had her brought to the chateau and flogged. The Countess de Berry got her maids to seize a rival and flog her. There was also, it is said, a good deal of flagellation of a more or less erotic character. An old French custom was to flog all the children of the house on Innocent's Day. It was supposed to impress upon them the fate of the children in King Harold's Day but was clearly just a reminder for the coming year of the penalty of misdeeds. From this, Granet says, young ladies get a pleasant custom of raiding each other's bedrooms on that day and flogging their*friends in bed. We can be sure that there was neither remorse nor anger in this case. The story is told of a man who coveted his wife's maid but was jealously watched by his wife. The maid was faulty, and on "Innocents" Day the man proposed that he should take a whip to the girl's bedroom and chastise her; and to this the wife foolishly consented.

It was much the same in every country. The Spaniards did even more flagellating than the French but they usually did it with that blend of gracefulness, pity, and vice which was characteristic of the country. Religious processions in Spain and Spanish America generally included flagellants but the practice was degenerating into the hire of a few toughs to flog themselves for pay as we still find in Seville. I mentioned in an earlier chapter how young men in love used to join these groups in order to impress ladies who watched from the balconies. It became one of the accepted methods of courting, and while some youths twanged guitars and crooned under the lady-love's balcony others flogged themselves. It seems to be this that Butler had in mind when he wrote in *Hudibras*:

> Why may not whipping have as good
> A grace, performed in time and mood,
> With comely movement and by art
> Raise passion in a lady's heart?

Granet says:

> Amongst the Spaniards they so generally considered the part of the human body of which we are treating here as the properest to bear ill-usage that in every place there is commonly some good friar who makes his posteriors censurable for the sins of the whole parish, and who, especially as he has been fed for that purpose, flogs himself (or at least tells his customers that he has done so). Hence the common Spanish saying, which is mentioned in the history of Friar Gerundide Compazes: "I am as badly off as the friar's rear."

This, of course, refers to Spain in the 18th Century. At the beginning of the 19th Napoleon's troops entered Spain, and these pious old customs were rudely shaken. The long series of popular revolutions and the triumph of liberalism and radicalism made the atmosphere still more unfavorable to them. Whether Franco has restored them to some extent I cannot say, but until quite recent years rich Britons and Americans at considerable expense went to see the hired mummery (including a few flagellants) of the Holy Week processions at Seville.

I need not examine every country. Germany was familiar with flagellation and almost led, as I will tell in the next chapter, in erotic flogging. Austria was the same, and we read with pleasure how one of its archduchesses of the 17th Century who was pressed to marry Philip of Spain had the Jesuit priest who importunately urged it flogged by her servants. The Swedes had some quaint customs. Cooper at all events says that down to his day (1870) women who were to be flogged were enclosed in copper sheaths which left only the back and the buttocks exposed. The lash was presumably heavy but, of course, the broad base of a Swedish woman could take a lot of punishment. Granet tells a curious story of whipping in Denmark. For any technical fault during a royal hunt the culprit had to be flogged. He knelt before the king and "two gentlemen removed the skirts of his coat and the king, taking a long wand in his hand, laid a certain number of blows upon the culprit's breeches, while the members of the hunt with brass horns and the hounds with loud barking proclaimed the King's Justice." The Dutch, who were familiar with the use of the lash in their eastern and African dependencies, continued to use it vigorously, and it is hardly necessary to say that the Russians wielded the knout as savagely as ever until the revolutionary movements of the present century intimidated the nobles.

CHAPTER XIV. EROTIC FLAGELLATION

Deeper than the irony of nearly all moralists in their toleration of the semi-savagery of flogging century after century, even consecrating it to religious use, is the fact that after it had remained throughout the period of civilization a "corrective" of vice it has become in our time little used except as a stimulation of vice. In this I put together the punitive and the theological uses of flagellation as means of promoting virtue, and both are now almost abandoned while the morbid use of it as a provocative of sexual feeling has certainly grown in modern times.

I know no more singular happening in the whole immense field of man's aberrations and stupidities during his slow climb to that level of intelligence which we call civilization. Even when men hardly had such a conception as virtue, and the king, the lord, the master or the parent spoke only of vindicating his authority, the aim of the custom was in large part moral intimidation. The culprit was warned not to repeat his misdeeds: others were taught what the price of misconduct would be. From this primitive conception the theologian or medicine-man easily deduced that the gods, being super-monarchs, must punish violations of their commands even more severely than mortal monarchs do, and it is one of the many arguments against the claim that religion is a guide to conduct that the higher the religion rose, as theologians measure such things, the more vicious was the conception of the divine vengeance. It seemed to the ancient Semite, whether Babylonian or Jew, and even the early Egyptians, since for 2,000 years they did not believe in the immortality of men, that the gods punish misconduct by sending upon a man one or other of the temporary afflictions, from boils to colic, of secular life. This raised the grave problem of the prosperity of the wicked and the misfortunes of pious folk, so in the next phase of the advance of religion, the Persian, the idea of punishment in an invisible world and a more agonizing form than ever was developed. This most repellent of religious aberrations to that time was adopted by Christianity and, with all its grave social consequences ,was imposed upon nearly the whole area of civilization.

The remorseful self-flagellation of the penitent or the prospective self-flagellation of the saint was a fairly logical deduction from this. Even a thousand lashes of a cruel whip seemed a low price to pay for escaping the sentence of hell. It suited the Church to discover that lighter austerities, such as giving substantial alms to the Church (the clergy) or making a pilgrimage to Rome (and pouring coins upon its altars) would suffice; and indeed, as we saw, the Church was always suspicious of the efficiency of any means of evading the divine anger which brought no grist to its own mill and which dispensed with the services of the clergy. Hence the short run and precarious life of Flagellant movements. If the Church imposed, or permitted monastic founders to impose, flogging upon monks and nuns we must remember, not only that they had no money but that they were supposed to be chastising the flesh to prevent sin rather than doing penance for serious sins committed.

You will find it difficult to discover a modern theologian who explains why, if the austerities of the saints were so sweet in the sight of God, it has been found advisable to abandon or to humanize them in modern times. The best outstanding example of serious self-flagellation was, as far as I can discover, the famous Parisian preacher, Father Lacordaire, a Dominican friar of about a century ago. His sermons, of which we have many volumes, show that he was no ignorant fanatic like Francis of Assisa, yet he was a great self-torturer. "Before the ashes of Voltaire were cold," says his pious biographer, "he restored in his own life all the virtuous truculence of the holier folk of the Middle Ages." As he was head of his monastery he could order the monks under his charge to tie him to a post and lay on mercilessly. He encouraged them to kick him and spit on him. He used to smile through it all and say: "Oh, if people only knew what a joy it is to be scourged for a loved one." It is another illustration of the tortuosity of the religious mind.° Normally, the "loved one" offers, if a whipping is unavoidable, to suffer it instead of the man who loves him, and the conception of "the gentle Jesus" taking pleasure in a man undergoing these painful or humiliating experiences seems to have appealed little to Lacordaire's own monks. Doubtless they read out of the accommodating modern book of rules that this was one of the saintly practices that are "to be admired rather than imitated."

Self-flagellation in a modern monastery is a farce. It is not worth inquiring how many rules of monks and nuns still prescribe it for I had experience of it and do not take it seriously. In the last century I lived 12 years in a Franciscan monastery and "taking the discipline" was one of the most innocent and ridiculous of our hypocrisies. Twice a week after supper the friars retired to their "cells" for the purpose. The brown robe of the friar has a thick head and shoulder piece and hood, and this one was obliged to draw over the head, which left one's back still comfortably covered with the thick brown tunic and the woollen shirt underneath it. The rope that ties this together at the waist is double and hangs to the ground in two knotted cords. To the faithful they probably look grim enough, but it was a sheer comedy swinging one of these cords across one's shoulders for two or three minutes while the superior at the end of the corridor recited a short psalm in a voice that carried to every cell. There was a rumor that one of the older friars was deputed to creep from door to door, to report any brother whose strokes could not be heard. But the whole thing was just a practice that edified the people when they were told about it. You could not have hurt yourself if you had tried, and nobody did try or was expected to do so.

It seems to be the same in the Jesuit and all other religious congregations. The thousand-year practice has degenerated into a silly little rite with no effect and no meaning whatever. Needless to say that there is no more erotic stimulation in it than there is in a remedy for the toothache, yet, as I said, no modern theologian condescends to explain how in a Church which never changes its principles and scorns to accommodate itself to our age a principle which every theologian and wise man of the Middle Ages adopted as unquestionable—the theory that God particularly loves mortals to torture themselves—has become as toothless as an old lion. Rome never changes. Monks still scourge themselves, the Catholic public are told; and they pay up.

In the jails, armies, and navies of civilized countries the practice has fallen into almost equal disrepute, but as this part of the world is not ruled by sacred moralists the practice has, with a few exceptions, been frankly abandoned and denounced as a semi-barbarous blunder. It has not been preserved in a soft and absurd form in order to save the faces of the blunderers. A mere statesman can afford to be honest—at least about the blunder of other statesmen. His infallibility is personal, not official and hereditary. The cat or cane is now rarely used, except in the East, though the use of it was recently restored in Chicago to check the great increase of crime. There are difficulties in a stage of transition between a crude old world and a world in which soldiers and sailors are treated as citizens with their own job to do, but it does not seem that the abandonment of flogging has led to more misconduct or mutiny than there was in the days when military "discipline" required that the soldier should be treated like a mule. Few men in authority are slower than military commanders to abandon old traditions and admit errors in them, yet few of them seem to regret the days when a dozen strokes were supposed to make a man more docile or more useful.

In the schools of the chief civilized countries all corporal punishment has now been generally abandoned. Teachers themselves are commonly unaware that almost down to a century ago flogging or caning of the nude buttocks, often before the whole school, was considered as normal a part of school life as communal prayers and much more normal than providing even comparatively decent sanitary arrangements. Instead of advertising for private schools at which a "difficult" boy or girl gets his or her stern tanned parents are apt to take a master or mistress to court the moment some spoiled darling complains that an exasperated teacher has boxed its ears or laid a ruler across the upper part of its back. Long debates at teachers' conferences have ended in a general agreement that corporal punishment is not necessary and is therefore a crude error of earlier days. So passes one of the most characteristic pieces of the wisdom of our fathers, in spite of its support in the Bible: "Spare the rod and spoil the child." It is ironic to reflect that not much more than a century ago the masters of schools for "the sons of gentlemen" were almost as familiar with the posteriors as with the faces of their pupils; that young ladies of 17 had at least their skirts lifted for punishment; and that visitors of mature years used to intrigue or pay to be admitted to enjoy the show.

In all these cases the practice of flagellation has retreated before the advance of law. As the law-maker still shows considerable reluctance to cross the threshold of the home we find there the last retreat of the lash. During the war there was a trial in Britain of a married couple, both churchgoers and Bible readers, who had received two boy refugees from London into their home. The boys were certainly young toughs of a bad type—in other words, they came from a bad environment—but the guardians beat them so cruelly with heavy straps and sticks that one of them died and this led to an inquiry. The child is still not protected, as the wife now is, by a law that it may not be beaten with a stick thicker than a man's thumb. There is, of course, nothing like the widespread cruelty of former times. Our immense literature about the treatment of children, which practically always opposes corporal punishment, has had a salutary effect on parents and formed a generally sound public opinion. The circulation of such literature is, however, always restricted, and doubtless the cane or the strap still swings merrily in countless homes.

The question is often raised by experts whether the corporal punishment of children is ever necessary. I hesitate to pronounce either way. I have reared four children without ever laying a hand on them or speaking angrily to them, and I am not one of the sweetest-tempered of mortals. I have known many homes where the father had the same ideal but the mother nagged him because he would not thrash the children at night for misconduct during the day. In most of these cases there would be no need of punishment if the mother were patient and tactful. She replies, naturally, that the father's experience of children is short and pleasant compared with hers, yet most folk must have noticed that women commonly relieve their own feelings by their slaps or find "I'll tell your father" an evasion of the task of studying the little problems of the child. Some experiences, however, prevent me from saying dogmatically that such punishment is never needed. It is enough that the flagellation of such dependents as servants, apprentices, etc., has been suppressed, and in the home it is yielding to saner methods of correction.

In short, it is now recognized that the vast amount of flogging that took place in nearly every department of life during the last 3,000 or more years was a barbaric practice maintained on a sheer moral aberration. There was, as I said, plenty of it in pre-Christian Roman civilization but there were many protests and in the last century of paganism there was much less cruelty. From the 12th to the 18th Century there was more flogging than ever, and the religious moralists who were, we are now told, building up our modern civilization not only did not protest but consecrated flogging. Even in the schools which spread over Europe once more after the 11th Century flogging was worse in the ancient Roman schools. I have no doubt that Orbilius and other Roman masters who were notorious for flogging often laid the ferule across a boy's buttocks, but nothing is said about nudity, and such things as schools for young ladies or for youths of 16 to 18 with the crude practice of stripping were unknown. It was just because the lash was practically confined to the slave world and a flogging conferred the mark of legal and social "infamy" that the earlier Christian ascetics did not include self-flagellation among their peculiar practices.

But the most ironic feature of the history of flagellation is, as I said, that while Christianity maintained and made more common than ever this implement of ancient barbarism on the ground that it not only promoted virtue by intimidation and helped to preserve in the individual who had the moral strength to use it on himself the choicest virtue in the ethical bouquet, purity, the modern world is in some quarters taking it up precisely as an aid to unchastity. At all events most writers on sex believe that the erotic use of the lash has increased during the last hundred years. Possibly we have some influence of a fallacy that often vitiates comparison of conduct in different ages. Many writers forget that you cannot justly compare conduct in different centuries unless the literature of one century tells you as much about conduct at that time as the literature of the other does. It is one of the chief weaknesses of the familiar practice of contrasting pagan vice and Christian virtue that we have few Latin books that tell us about *general* conduct from, say, 200 B.C. to 300 A.D. Few read even these; and, while a few serious characters in them are picturesque enough to get into history, even the keen social student who has a good knowledge of Latin finds it difficult to deduce the *average* moral character. As far as erotic flagellation is concerned even the most diligent classical scholars have found only two or three references to it in the course of 500 years. It appears from these that there was a practice of beating the pubic region with green nettles, but the extent of it is quite unknown, and that certain street entertainers amongst the workers depended largely upon prurience for their fun. Flogging on the nude stern is hardly mentioned. In the Lupercalia the priests did not flagellate the women—and these do not seem to have been stripped until Chrisian times—but flicked them with a strip of hide as they ran past.

For the next stretch of European history (about 400 to 1050—the Dark Age) the literature is, apart from the ponderous works of a few theologians, so crude and scanty that it is almost useless to a social student. Lists of sins which survive suggest an incredible grossness amongst the mass of the people, the priests, and the monks, and the chroniclers confirm the impression and extend it to the bishops, archbishops, and popes. It seems that, although crude and indescribable aphrodisiacs are mentioned, there was not much need for erotic stimulation in the Dark Age.

From 1050 onward we see it increasingly adopted as the secret instrument of virtue as well as an indispensable piece of school furniture, a fearful weapon of civil justice and of the Inquisition, and the favorite implement of every type of master. Literature increases and gives us a broader view of character. The troubadour literature in particular reflects a life of such abounding sexual vitality that we hardly expect to find much trace of perverse practices (except pederasty, which is common) or any writer taking an interest in such things. The cases I quoted from Pico della Mirandola do suggest that during the Italian Renaissance and the great growth of city life the practice of erotic flogging increased, as we should expect, and the fact that the first writer on the subject, the Dutch Meibom, finds more instances in the world about him than in a thousand years of history confirms us in thinking that it is the recording, not the occurrence, of such things that is uncommon.

From the 16th Century onward the sex-motif is heard more and more clearly in connection with flagellation. The pious and dour Flagellants degenerate into the processions of the morbid Henry III, and his pansies. Such incidents as Father Cornelius and his girl penitents, Mlle. Cordiere sticking her stern out of a window to be lashed by a Jesuit when the clergy incarcerate her, the Bonjour priests, the pseudo-Flagellants meeting in the dark, and so on, stink of sex. The writers of fiction and humorists are quite alive to this. In his collection of "Fables" Lafontaine has an amusing story, "The Pair of Spectacles," much softened in the English translation, that reflects the general popular interest in such matters. In a certain convent a number of nuns were found to be in what modern journalists call an interesting condition, and the abbess suspected that some young man of effeminate appearance had passed himself off as a woman and entered the community. She called the nuns together and ordered them to strip. The author seems to imply that she wanted to detect him for her own satisfaction, and he, in language that I may not translate, invents an accident to her spectacles at the critical moment. The nuns dragged the young man into the garden, stripped him, and tied him to a tree for flogging. They had, however, forgotten their disciplines or scourges, and when they ran back to the convent for them, a passing miller heard the young man's laments and gladly changed places with him. His belief in his attractiveness miscarried, and the nuns gave him a sound flogging.

The sex-note pervades all European literature of the 17th and 18th centuries and is a true reflection of life. There can be no doubt that masters often found a sexual satisfaction, doubtless often vague or marked by other feelings, in whipping boys and mistresses in whipping girls. In modern times this is apt to be described as sadism but strictly speaking the sadist is a man who is sexually excited by inflicting cruelty and possibly requires that stimulus. The feeling in these cases seems to have been mixed and to have been aroused as much by the performance on nude buttocks as by any consciousness of inflicting pain. Some, in fact, hold that there was a certain measure of sexual pleasure in flagellation even when it was not cruel and not in the nude. The French *Grande Encyclopedie,* which was at one time much superior to the *Britannica* but had to be as, though its writers were largely skeptics, the political authority in France at the time was Catholic, said in its article on flagellation:

> Not only is it still the rule of several congregations of monks and nuns but it brings to the intimates of the cloister an intermediate relief or a precious condiment to relieve, by sensations of a weird mysticism, the monotony and boredom of a contemplative life.

This, however, is rather fanciful. The modern monastic discipline is just a piece of dead ritual that bores rather than relieves boredom. And if the sex-note appears more and more frequently in connection with flagellation from the 18th Century onward we must not conclude at once that erotic flagellation greatly increased. What certainly did increase was legal prosecution for sexual offenses or for assaults with a suggestion of a sex element and, naturally, the journalistic recording of such cases. I quoted a case of a master of a London workhouse being prosecuted for a practice of punishing with his own hand the young girls in his charge by slapping them on their nude little hemispheres; also the case of a rector of an important city-church who was prosecuted because he was in the habit of inflicting the same punishment on his wife's maid, a plump young person of 16 or 17. No notice would have been taken of such things in an earlier period when nude sterns were a joke and flogging them a pleasant spectacle.

There is another element to be taken into account from the end of the 18th Century. Lords and masters, the habitual flagellators, were apt to have their conduct called into question after the French Revolution. There is a case of an aristocratic British officer, Lt. General Sir

Eyre Coote, being prosecuted in the Lord Mayor's Court at London in 1815, and such a prosecution could hardly have been undertaken or received so much unpleasant publicity at an earlier date. The fact that it made a sensation was largely due, I imagine, to surprise at the audacity of the London police arresting "an officer and a gentleman" for what most folk still regarded as a trivial offense or an amusing eccentricity.

Christ's Hospital in the city of London had, as usual, a medical school attached to it, for preparatory as well as strictly medical lessons. The honorable and gallant gentleman (in the language of the time) visited it in an unofficial hour and joked with the boys. He brought the conversation round to their floggings and, after cautiously sounding a group of them, offered a few boys (probably of 16 or 17) 30 cents—then equal to about a dollar—each if they would lower their pants and allow him to give them six strokes of the lash. They agreed, and he went on to pay them to do the same to himself. But the porter of the hospital had heard the bargain and reported it to the authorities, and these informed the police. His attorney tried to pass it off as a joke in bad taste but the charge was pressed and heard in the chief court of the city.

Cooper, who reports this, tells us that at the time there were Whipping Clubs, both in England and Germany, in which friends and even brothers and sisters met to give each other the birch, which they had learned to appreciate in their school days. Unfortunately the author gives no reference or details, as is common in his gossipy work, and I have not been able to find any confirmation of this interesting statement. It suggests not only a piquant new chapter in the history of flagellation but seems to indicate, in conjunction with the above cases, that there was an appreciable development of erotic flagellation. Most writers speak of the development of sadism (the infliction of cruelty in order to excite one's own sexual instincts) and masochism (submitting to punishment for the same purpose) but it is not clear that in any of these cases the flogging went so far as actual infliction of pain. No doubt the works of the Marquis de Sade, which were now published, tended to provoke morbid practices, but they were then little known in either England or Germany; and, of course, Masoch, who gives his name to masochism (passive erotic flagellation), belongs to a later date.

These things do not properly concern me here, nor need I inquire if and why the changed conditions of life in the 19th Century led to a growth of sexual perversions. It is enough that nude flagellation was increasingly regarded as inducing a pleasurable sexual feeling, and this is quite commonly connected with experience of flogging in schooldays or in the early home. This is hinted by Pico della Mirandola and Meibom in the works I quoted and is a common note in modern cases. A passage in Rousseau's *Confessions* is always quoted in this connection. To call anything about Rousseau typical is risky. His peculiar temperament—"nature broke the mold when it made me," he says rather conceitedly—gives individual shades of difference to all his experiences. He describes himself as extremely sensual but having all his life a horror of loose women, and he was not in any sense whatever pervert. His story is interesting, however, as confirming that bottom slapping or birching in childhood is often the cause of an inclination in later years to erotic flagellation.

He tells in his first chapter how in early years he had a governess, Mdlle. Lambercier, a strict young lady of 30 years, who chastised him with the rod. He felt that this was a disgrace but was a curiously pleasant experience, and, while he did not wish to offend her by misbehaving again, he longed to be put across her knee again. "For," he says, "I found in the pain, even in the shame, an element of sensuality which left me with more desire than fear to receive the treatment again. It is true that since doubtless some precocious sex instinct was involved in it, if her brother had given me the treatment I should not have found it pleasant." He managed to get a farther dose of the treatment, but the young lady noticed something in his eye that made her decide not to do it again. He naturally knew nothing about the effect on herself and does not suggest that there was any. However, "to that time I had slept in her room, in winter in her bed, and I was now put in another room and had the honor, which I did not want, of being treated as a big boy." The experience influenced him for life. Although he had "a blood burning with sensuality almost from birth," he did not, when he reached maturity, look for the usual satisfaction—he had had puritanical parents and education—but when he saw beautiful women he enjoyed in imagination the delights of being put across their knees. He, as I said, abhorred prostitutes. He never confessed his feeling to any woman but all his life he brooded over the pleasure of "being put across the knees of an imperious mistress."

We must, as I said, not regard anything in Rousseau as typical but in most of the few recorded individual cases the patient traces his longing back to such chastisement in childhood or the early teens. In his *Psychology of Sex* (vol. VII) Havelock Ellis gives a case at great length and mainly in the words of the lady herself. She describes herself as a strong and rather stout woman of 37 who seemed to her friends entirely normal. It seems to be suggested that she was a well-known woman. She read Ellis's work, got into communication with him, and gave him a long memorandum on her secret experiences.

She was married but relations with her husband never gave her the normal satisfaction. She let herself go in day dreams, and these took the form more and more of a desire for flagellation. She had, she said, been often and severely whipped by her father, and it is fairly clear that the vague pervasive sex feeling in which she was left by the incomplete intercourse with her husband caused her thoughts to revert to this early experience. More and more she dreamed of the pleasure of being whipped. She flogged herself severely, nude, but this gave her no satisfaction. Her favorite dream was that she eloped with a groom and was heavily flogged by him. She had only the average woman's knowledge about sex and did not understand that the feeling that pervaded her was making her strain after an orgasm that never came. At last she got into contact with a man who wrote a letter about whipping to some paper, and his rather crude and blunt letters further stimulated her. At last, though a refined and cultivated woman and the man was of a rough type, she spent a night with him at a hotel, though simply for the purpose of being flogged; and he was of the type that enjoys active flagellation. "I enjoyed it thoroughly," she says, "though I was black and blue for a fortnight." Soon after she came into contact with Ellis and he succeeded in diverting or dissipating her morbid craving.

I do not agree with much that sexologists read into these things. Some suggest that these people see the rod as a symbol and the reddening of the skin as a symbol of blushing. Others think that there is an esthetic element in a man's desire to flog women. But for these matters I must refer the reader to works on sex. We recognize today that there is a diffused feeling of sex—more or less secondarily—concentrated in the lips and breasts—as well as the specifically localized sensation. We know also that in such cases as the above a lowered vitality of the sex glands prevents complete satisfaction, and the vague general feeling leads to excessive irritation and morbid practices such as erotic flagellation. Some experts consider that only one man or woman in a hundred is excited by flagellation. Havelock Ellis, who has collected the largest amount of information, emphatically disputes that, but all the positive evidence given in the works of sexologists leaves us uncertain of the extent of the practice. One recent French writer, quoted in Dr. Robinson's *Encyclopedia Sexualis*, recommends impotent fathers to seek a remedy by flogging their children, and Dr. Robinson says that in certain periodicals in Paris one "frequently" comes across such advertisements as:

Elderly gentleman interested in the works of the Marquis de Sade would like to meet young lady interested in the works of Sacher Masoch.

I doubt the accuracy of the word "frequently" but in the words of Krafft-Ebing and other sexologists there is enough evidence, particularly in regard to loose houses, to justify my statement that while the lash or birch has fallen into disrepute as a punisher of delinquency or guardian of virtue, erotic flagellation has increased.

NOTES AND COMMENTS

By E. Haldeman-Julius

Is Professor Einstein, Nobel prize winner and co-worker in the early theoretical research that made possible the splitting of the atom, a Socialist?

Yes, Albert Einstein is a Socialist. But how strange that his declaration of support for Socialism was ignored by the capitalistic press—that supposedly free press that's always criticizing the Russian press because it isn't like the Wall Street press. *The New York Times, The Kansas City Star,* Colonel McCosmic's *Chicago Tribune,* the Hearst organs of piety and righteousness, the Patterson gutter newspapers, the Gannett string, and the rest of the journalistic pimps of Big Business refused to print a word of Einstein's statement. It surely is *news* when a scientist, mathematician, thinker and public figure of the stature of Einstein issues a statement in support of the philosophy of Socialism, and yet the newspapers preferred to ignore it. Here's the Einstein statement that the Kept Press refused to print:

"I am convinced, on the whole, that in a state with a socialized economy, better prospects exist for the individual to attain that maximum of freedom consistent with the welfare of all society.

"The reason: In a soundly managed society, everyone works for the satisfaction of common needs rather than for the profit of a propertied minority. The problem of a more or less equal divison of labor can, in my belief, be solved only in a planned economy, and not under a system of free enterprise where the industrialist is compelled to reduce the number of workers as far as possible and increase to the maximum the productivity of labor. Under those conditions, every invention of a labor-saving machine increases chronic unemployment. Out of this arises growing unemployment and economic insecurity which also means loss of freedom, insofar as freedom is affected by economic conditions.

"The socialization of the more important means of production is, however, still not socialism, even though it is a prerequisite of it. Part and parcel of socialism is also that concentrated power be effectively controlled by the citizenry, so that the planned economy benefits the entire people, so that the road be kept open for all—in accordance with their natural qualifications—to the most important posts. Only constant political struggle and vigilance can create that situation and maintain it.

"Therefore, conditions for the attainment of individual freedom for the majority are more favorable in a socialist state than in an economic system based upon private ownership."

*   *   *

How fast does Walter Winchell speak? His rate is 210 words a minute, including all flashes. This, for no sane reason, reminds me of a sky-writer who makes his living 10,000 feet up writing "Pepsi-Cola." Recently, over Kansas City, he turned out his masterpiece—each letter distinct—but as he finished, a dozen transport planes flew straight through and ruined his artistic creation. Outraged, seething with anger, the sky-writer rose another 2,000 feet and dashed off this expletive: "O----!"

*   *   *

An advertising copywriter for the Otis Elevator Company lost his job because he suggested this slogan: "Good to the Last Drop."

*   *   *

Walter Winchell, who expects to have a book issued soon, has asked his publisher to supply each buyer with a free telegraph key which is to be rattled at the end of each sentence.

*   *   *

Erasmus (1466-1536), Dutch scholar and author, in Little Blue

Book 1266: "They (the friars) are called fathers and they often are."

* * *

Irwin Erdman, U. S. teacher and writer: "There is practically no evidence for the existence of God."

* * *

Jack English, American Catholic writer and teacher: "For the truth is that no American Catholic has ever turned out an important novel. The American Catholic's meager contribution to contemporary literature, especially to fiction, is so apparent."

* * *

Albert Einstein, scientist: "Do I think religion will help promote peace? It has not done so up to now."

* * *

Robert C. Benchley, while making a survey of the educational backgrounds of movie stars, came to the written reply of Lana Turner, which opened: "I was educated by a private tooter."

* * *

I have just seen my first copy of *Vanguard*, dated April 7, 1946. This readable, informative, forward-looking, progressive, intelligently radical organ of democratic Socialism is the English daily newspaper of the Radical Democratic Party, printed and published at Delhi, India. *Vanguard* contains my article, "The Problem of India," which appeared in The Freeman. The editor of *Vanguard* added this note to the reprinted editorial:

"The American Freeman is a Rationalist monthly paper which has been waging a relentless war against all reactionary tendencies in our democratic civilization. In politics The American Freeman has always presented a militant anti-Fascist front and championed the cause of the American common man as against the monopoly capitalists usurping power in government in the name of democracy.

"Mr. E. Haldeman-Julius, editor of The American Freeman, is also the editor and proprietor of the world-famous Little Blue Books and other E. Haldeman-Julius publications. A veritable galaxy of front-rank scholars, philosophers, novelists, and journalists head his enviable list of contributors. His writers include men of first class intelligence and international reputation, like Joseph McCabe, H. G. Wells, Bertrand Russell, L. M. Birkhead, Upton Sinclair, Clarence Darrow, Isaac Goldberg, and a host of others."

Will people heed Albert Einstein who don't read Merrill's lucubrations on atomic energy in The American Freeman? The great philosopher of Relativity wants a fund of $200,000 raised for the purpose of acquainting the public with the imminent danger of annihilation which humanity faces. "The unleashed power of the atom," declared Einstein, "has changed everything save our modes of thinking, and thus we drift toward unparalleied catastrophe." Not so many years before the war, Einstein was extremely dubious about the ability of man to ever harness the stupendous energy called for by his equivalence of matter and energy formula. Now our Navy Department hints about developing a weapon more terrible than the atom bomb.

* * *

How the nuns and priests turned out at that election in Italy! His Holiness is going into politics with a vengeance. No wonder our Presbyterians are worried about U. S. representatives at the Vatican.

* * *

Priscilla Prissy-Pratt's 7-year-old nephew was listening to his teacher's health lecture, in which she warned her pupils against kissing animals or birds. "Teacher," said the boy, "I know it's dangerous because my aunt, Priscilla Prissy-Pratt, used to kiss her dog. It died."

* * *

Rita Hayworth, whose real name is Margarita Cansini, is threatening to sue a Hollywood singer because she's capitalizing on her name. The singer's using the name Rita Haywood, but her real name happens to be Rita Haywood.

*

Jonathan Edwards, American preacher (1703-1758): "The sight of hell's torments will exalt the happiness of the saints forever."

* * *

Max Eastman: "I would define Religion as a belief that there is Something in the objective world, aside from other people, to which you can direct your emotions of love and adoration, and that you will be helped by loving this Something. If this definition is acceptable, I am prepared to defend the proposition that Religion is a hindrance to progress. The idea that we are all children of God, and that we must love God with all our strength uses up just that much love which we might turn to the loving of our neighbor."

* * *

Judge Dunn, Supreme Court of Illinois: "The free enjoyment of religious worship includes the freedom not to worship."

* * *

Theological crap, as dished up by the Rev. Father Owen Dudley, Roman Catholic Missionary Society: "A miracle is not a violation of the laws of nature, because when Jesus walked on the water the law of gravity was not violated. Its effect was suspended, so far as Christ's body was concerned, and a greater divine power came into play."

* * *

Anything can happen in Hollywood. Take the case of an important preview of a new film, adapted from a novel by a popular writer. The writer asked who wrote the story, and was told that he did, that the movie company had taken it from his book. The author was surprised. He commented that he wouldn't have known it and suggested that it would make an excellent novel. He then asked permission to use the idea and was told to go right ahead, so long as he gave the company an option on the film rights.

* * *

John Stuart Mill (1806-1873), English economist, logician, and philosopher, in Little Blue Book Nos. 177, 211 and 615: "A large proportion of the noblest and most valuable moral teaching has been the work, not only of men who did not know, but of men who knew and rejected the Christian faith." . . . "The world would be astonished if it knew how great a proportion of its brightest ornaments, of those most distinguished even in popular estimation for wisdom and virtue are complete skeptics in religion." . . . "The ne plus ultra of wickedness is embodied in what is commonly presented to mankind as the creed of Christianity." . . . "Modern morality is derived from Greek and Roman sources, not from Christianity." . . . " "God is a word to ex-

press, not our ideas, but the want of them." . . . "No belief which is contrary to truth can be really useful." . . . "My father taught me that the question, 'Who made me?' cannot be answered, since it immediately suggests the further question, 'Who made God?' "

* * *

Jean Meslier: "We have every reason to believe that no religion has the advantage of being true."

* * *

George Meredith (1828-1909), English novelist: "When I was quite a boy I had a spasm of religion which lasted six weeks. But I never since have swallowed the Christian fable."

* * *

Charles H. Hogan, author of "The Kansas City Star: Truman is a man running a gent's furnishing store in a bum neighborhood. He's a small-town Rotarian. No, he's merely a Kiwanian."

* * *

A night club manager, to discourage homos from patronizing the joint, put up this sign: "Men Not Admitted Without Female Escorts."

* * *

Harpo Marx: "I am at work on a musical life of Debussy, to be called 'Debussy Debunked.' "

* * *

From a book ad in The Kansas City Star: "Critics recommend 'The Snake Pit,' the surprisingly charming, humorous story of a year in an insane alysum!"

* * *

Patsy O'Bang, to bartender: "Now, friend, if you should happen to give me the bum's rush earlier than other nights, I should be able to wind up with a good night's sleep."

* * *

Robert C. Benchley: "Ferenc Molnar, when he was a journalist, said a certain sensationally thin newspaper man, when born, was taken in hand by the nurse, who threw away the child but kept the umbilical cord."

* * *

Ferenc Molnar, the Hungarian-Jewish playwright, just before he pulled out of Nazi Europe for New York, said: "A Jew should never own more property than he can jump quickly over a fence with."

* * *

Overheard: "I'm sure my husband will love me when my hair is gray, because he's loved me when it was every other color."

* * *

Waitress, to patron who has left a 5c tip: "Whatcha tryin' to do, bub, seduce me?"

* * *

Bartender: "Had a preacher guy in here a while ago and he ordered a glass of milk, but I made a mistake and served an egg-nog. He drank it to the last drop, raised his eyes upward and said: 'Lord, what a cow!'"

* * *

The bride's old man: "The reason my new son-in-law marched up to the altar as though he had lead in his pants is because he did."

* * *

Old man to his care-worn wife, as he points to the cemetery across the street: "Ma, every time I look across the street I keep thinking of our dear daughter layin' there in that cemetery, and it sure makes me very sad. It makes me so sad, Ma, that sometimes I even wish she was dead."

* * *

Patsy O'Bang: "To err is human, but it feels divine."

* * *

The loving was so torrid, it moved a woman at the movie to poke her husband with her elbow and say: "When are you going to make love like that?" His reply: "I happen to know that that fellow is getting $365,750 a year for doing it."

* * *

From a recipe: "Steal four ounces of butter . . ."

* * *

There was a Berlin banker (before Hitler) named Herr Shwantzputz, who telephoned another Berlin banker, whom he did not like but had to see on a business matter. The man, whose name was Shicedrek, said he'd have to look through his engagement book before he could make an appointment. Shwantzputz heard the surf of the pages being ruffled in Shicedrek's book. No free time in January, February, or March. The third of April was his first free afternoon. "On April third," said Herr Shwantzputz, "I have a funeral."

* * *

Patsy O'Bang, to his latest passion, a tall, gorgeous blonde: "I have everything ready for a grand night—a lovely apartment, a case of good likker, credit with the confused hotel manager—all for tonight. Will you come?" The girl: "Give me the night to think it over."

* * *

Ferenc Molnar: "There was a dreadful man in Vienna named Haas, an inveterate first-nighter and a fountain of malice. At one opening, just before the curtain rose, somebody asked him a question, involving some esoteric family relationship, which he couldn't answer. The moment the first curtain came down, he rushed to his questioner. 'Your question cost me a sleepless first act,' he said. The remark killed the play."

* * *

Ferenc Molnar: "Opening nights in Budapest and Vienna were festive; the boxes would glitter with uniforms and tiaras. A Frau Baroness von Pollack was always present on these occasions. One time, after the curtain fell on a dingy play about poor people, the Baroness felt let down. 'It's no play for a premiere,' she said."

* * *

Mrs. Priscilla Prissy-Pratt wanted to get to the mailbox, but couldn't because a young woman's dog had reached there first. Not only did the dog make elaborate use of the mailbox post but he went in for a lengthy routine of investigation, seeming to use his nose in an attempt to identify every creature that had done business before. This irritated Mrs. Prissy-Pratt, but she tolerated this irritation for a few moments. More time passed. At least, her patience spent, she snapped: "Young lady, when your dog is through with that post, I'd like to use it."

* * *

Professor Patsy Bang, to a Harvard class that wasn't learning very fast: "If this class were to stand up and form a circle, I'd be liable to arrest under the federal statutes, because I'd be harboring a dope ring."

* * *

A reader doesn't like to see the Japanese called Japs. He thinks it's a racial insult. I don't agree. Jap is merely an abbreviation of Japanese, as Yank is a shorter form of Yankee. No insult is intended.

It isn't at all like nigger, wop, dago, hunk, greaser, and the like. But, I may be wrong. If so, set me right.

* * *

A colored girl complained in court that her ex-boy-friend had eloped with another girl, despite the fact that he'd promised to marry her. When the judge asked if she had anything in black and white to show for it, she replied: "Nope, just black is all."

* * *

Teacher, to history student: "You flunked your history test because your answer to the question, 'Why did the pioneers go into the wilderness?' was interesting from the standpoint of sanitation but it still was incorrect."

* * *

Girl friend, pouring a drink for a marine: "Say when, but don't say, 'any time after the first drink is O.K. by me.'"

* * *

Commercial slogan: "Cheeses That Pleases."

* * *

I've enjoyed the pleasures and satisfactions of modern plumbing for more than 50 years, but still I refuse to take it without comment. Every time I flush a toilet, I mutter: "That's a wonderful thing."

* * *

Bishop Beerbelch, described by Senator Gooseflesh: "The good bishop functions like most of us senators. The obvious he confuses at once. The crystal clear takes a little longer."

* * *

Pillar of a dying, debt-ridden church in a small town: "Our church isn't getting on very well, but thank the Lord, the others aren't doing any better."

* * *

Mrs. Jones: "I'm going to fire my new maid just as soon as she worries me down to 140 pounds."

* * *

Mark Twain, when he finished "Tom Sawyer Abroad," insisted that Dan Beard do the drawings for *St. Nicholas* magazine. The editor returned his artistic creations of Huck Finn, Tom Sawyer and others, his reason being that "it was excessively coarse and vulgar to depict them with bare feet." The artist conformed to the prissy editor's notions of propriety, pinching the toes of those grand vagabonds with shoes they never wore in life. Beard asked their mental forgiveness as he committed this little crime against the truth.

* * *

Patsy O'Bang: "Dr. Samuel Johnson was right when he said no man has the comforts in his own home that he can find at an inn."

* * *

Henry L. Mencken: "I never listen to the radio. I dislike the telephone. I prefer the Congressional Record to the newspapers. My price for going to a movie is $10,-000—cash in advance."

* * *

Oscar Wilde: "Know him? I know him so well I haven't spoken to him for 10 years."

* * *

Junius: "The man who is conscious of the weakness of his cause is interested in concealing it."

* * *

Shortly after being made a prince of the church, Cardinal Glennon stopped off in Ireland, where he died. His body was brought by airplane from Ireland to St. Louis, entirely at government expense. Citizens should ask their congressmen why the church is able to command such special privileges, and at the expense of the taxpayers.

* * *

Dr. Patsy O'Bang, world's greatest geneticist, in a Harvard lecture, reported that he was at work breeding home-broken mice.

* * *

Mickey Rooney: "O thou omnipotent, omniscient, omnipresent, all-seeing, ever-living, blessed Potentate, Lord God Jehovah! I am a self-made man. Yes—and I worship my creator."

* * *

Patsy O'Bang: "We shall come to an end some day, though we may never live to see it."

* * *

Bob Hope: "We must dare, and again dare, and forever dare."

* * *

Henry David Thoreau, in Little Blue Book 339: "I have three chairs in my house: one for solitude, two for friendship, three for society."

* * *

Goethe, in Little Blue Book 201: "There is nothing more terrible than energetic ignorance."

* * *

Critical crap from *The Washington Post*: "Sibylline by nature as in name is the young American choreographer, Sybil Shearer. who last evening closed and climaxed the excellant series of dance recitals presented by the Jewish Community Center. Beneath the humor of her lighter fancies, and pervading the very tissues of her exalted conceptions, is the divination of a seeress who perceives the potentials of a moment of time. She also knows the stillness of the body that parallels the silence of the mind—both receptive states of concentrated energy and incipient activity. The physical and the psychic elements of her being work in perfect accord."

* * *

Banker, to Patsy O'Bang: "If you're so smart, why aren't you rich like me?" Patsy O'Bang: "If you're so rich, why aren't you smart?"

* * *

Name of hash-house: Hilly-Billy-Grilly.

* * *

Movie actress, according to a *New Yorker* cartoon: "He's a perfect darling, of course. The only trouble is I'm not sure I want to start marrying yet."

* * *

Dr. Stephan Lackner, Santa Barbara, Calif.: "Bigots are getting accustomed to being shocked by the Haldeman-Julius publications."

* * *

Bertrand Russell: "Los Angeles represents the ultimate segregation of the unfit."

* * *

Groucho Marx, to buxom widow he loved: "You're so beautiful and so clever and so rich and so charming and so rich and so gracious and so rich and so intelligent and so rich."

* * *

W. C. Fields: "He's the kind of guy who'd milk his neighbor's cow through a crack in the fence."

* * *

Young and ambitious funeral director, to aged mourner at cemetary: "As you're 98, it's hardly worth going home."

* * *

Theodore Parker (1810-1860), American theologian: "The Bible sanctions slavery. So much the worse for the Bible." ... "The Scriptures are no finality to me. I do not believe there ever was a miracle or ever will be. I do not take the Bible nor the Church, nor even Jesus of Nazareth, for my master."

* * *

Betty Grable: "The time has come when all religious denominations must affirm that no public moneys shall be used for sectarian instruction; the time-honored principle of the separation of church and state must be again emphasized. If a church is not willing to support its own schools, it cannot come to the state for aid. I would go so far in the application of this principle as to be willing to see all our churches taxed as is other property. We have no right to tax unbelievers that churches may be maintained; no more right than they would have to tax churches for the support of infidel clubs."

* * *

Bears and gorillas don't do it, but fancy an ardent human lover hugging a woman to death! That happened lately, although Peter the Great, whose boisterous amatory behavior was the scandal of his time and ultimately killed him by ruining his prostate gland, was as innocent of that sort of homicide as an affectionate gorilla. The verdict is that the lover pressed too hard on a certain nerve in his beloved's neck. How come the waist of that unfortunate woman was just below her ears?

* * *

Mickey Rooney: "When all the world's at war, it's easy enough to be pleasant; but the person worth while is the one who can smile in a time of peace like the present."

* * *

The school directors of Jewell, Ore., anxious to give culture a lift, hired Colen McEwen as principal of the Mehalem Valley high school, with instructions to bust loose on literature but to be careful not to drag in "The Grapes of Wrath" and "Strange Fruit." When McEwen heard that he was to teach literature without literature, he said: "It is silly for the directors to dictate regarding the books that may or may not be used. I can't teach modern U. S. literature if I'm ordered not to use the books of novelists who in the course of great ealistic portrayals of life, present with fidelity the manners, morals and the speech of real people." The board insists that literature classes can be kept pure by being exposed to the works of Harold Bell Wright and William C. Douglas, two of America's foremost shovelers of literary crap. Culture is still on the bum in the schools.

In one of my recent articles I mentioned that the late Joseph Medill Patterson, publisher of *The New York Daily News,* had been one of the group of powerful figures in the field of publishing who had been converted to the Roman Catholic Church. Some readers questioned the assertion, saying that while it was true that Mrs. Luce had been won over to the One and Only Church, there was nothing to show that Patterson had gone the same way. *The New York Times,* in reporting Capt. Patterson's funeral, on May 30, 1946, said: "Capt. Roman T. Blatz, Roman Catholic Chaplain at Arlington, read the committal service."

What's our world coming to? Isn't God in his heaven? Fancy one of his tabernacles being sued for $20,000 by a 30-year member whose child fell into a baptismal tank and was injured! Was it because the presumably holy water of that particular tank had been drained off and that child was without benefit of a fluid which should prevent bones from being broken as conveniently as it washes sin away? It's just one of those things, perhaps, and comparable with a soldier's life being saved by a pocketbook packed with bills won at galloping dominos instead of a miraculous New Testament.

Undertaker, running down a competitor: "All right, all right, buy his casket for $50 less than this fine article, but I'm ready to bet that six months after they bury you your behind will be sticking out through the bottom."

The newest perfume in Moscow is labelled "Stalin's Breath."

Banker, to Groucho Marx: "Frankly, I'm worried about whether you can meet your note next month." Groucho: "Good! That's what I'm paying you interest for."

Robert C. Benchley: "Every newspaperman should work at least one year for Hearst to learn what not to do in journalism."

How the Man in the Street reacts to the demand that he do some thinking about atomic bombs: "What good does it do to talk about it?" "The big-shots in Washington will work that out." "Some defense will be found; there always has." "They won't dare use it." "The U. S. A. can always stay ahead of anybody else, so ishkibible." "If it's a secret all we have to do is keep it that way." "We've never lost a war, so why worry?" "We ought to bottle up all foreign scientists."

Said of Senator Gooseflesh: "He's sure to bring up a difficulty for every solution."

Clarence Darrow: "William Jennings Bryan ate like a man with a stowaway under his vest."

John Morley, English statesman and historian: "All religions die of one disease—that of being found out." . . . "Voltaire was a stupendous power." . . . "The system which begins by making mental indolence a virtue, and intellectual narrowness a part of sanctity, ends by putting a premium on hypocrisy." . . . "You (Christianity) have so debilitated the minds of men and women that many generations must come and go before Europe can throw off the yoke of your superstition. But we promise you they shall be years of strenuous battle." . . . "The great ship of your church (Christianity), once so stout and fair, has become a skeleton ship; it is a phantom bulk with warped planks and sere canvas; and you who work it are no more than the ghosts of dead men; and, at the hour when you seem to have reached the bay, down your ship will sink like lead or stone to the deepest bottom."

Customer: "What will you charge me for an unabridged dictionary that has a complete index?"

Lady Mary Mortley Montagu, English writer: "Priests can lie, and

the mob believe, all over the world."
... "Every honest person must condemn the quackery of all the churches."

* * *

Edouard Herriot, author, Freethinker, and former Premier of France: "Now that I have grown old, I have the feeling, when walking through a cemetary, that I am apartment-hunting."

Washington newspaper correspondents, in answering the question, "Who is the worst columnist?" agreed on Bob Hope.

* * *

Heywood Broun: "My favorite breakfast dish is not Wheaties or Crunchies or anything like that but ice cream and gin."

* * *

Soda jerk, to young woman: "If you want to learn to kiss I recommend dragging my heavy malted milk up a straw."

* * *

Heard on the beach: "My goodness, isn't that Fanny Brown over there?"

* * *

W. C. Fields: "I should like to debunk the fallacy of the old saying, 'All happiness is in the mind.' Some occasionally is in the stomach, and some frequently is some inches further down."

* * *

Montesquieu (1689-1755), French political scientist, jurist, and philosopher: "Churchmen are interested in keeping the people ignorant. I call piety a malady of the heart. The false notion of miracles comes of our vanity, which makes us believe we are important enough for the Supreme Being to upset Nature on our behalf."

* * *

Significant announcement by the chief of police of Miami, Fla.: "In the future, married women seeking a permit to purchase firearms must be accompanied by their husbands."

* * *

From General Motors' report to its stockholders: "$52,000,000 of the $88,000,000 cost of the 113-day strike was written off through federal income and excess-profits-tax adjustments." This means that the U. S. government was used in an effort to beat down the workers. Such tax deductions should be disallowed.

* * *

Barthold Georg Niebuhr (1776-1831), German historian and professor: "I would not overthrow the dead Church; but, if she fall, it will cause me no uneasiness."

Jawaharlal Nehru, Indian leader: "Religion is a killjoy." ... "The spectacle of what is called religion, or at any rate organized religion, in India and elsewhere, has filled us with horror, and I have frequently condemned it and wished to make a clean sweep of it."

Questions: "Which virgin was Christ's mother—the Virgin Mary or the King James virgin?" ... "Does the second curl in the pig's tail change the flavor of the meat?"

* * *

Bishop Beerbelch: "I believe poverty is necessary." Patsy O'Bang: "But is it necessary that it should forever remain in the same hands?"

Keith Preston: "The alienist finds you cracked and leaves you broke."

Overheard: "That guy knows he's always right because his automobile and house are the biggest in his neighborhood."

* * *

Mickey Rooney: "When you talk to people in lower income levels you find a large majority who wonder if the American capitalistic system is really right."

* * *

W. C. Fields: "The typical radio commercial fits into the show the way a riveting machine would fit into a symphony orchestra."

* * *

Thomas Mann: "The future belongs to socialistic democracy. I hope, and am convinced, that Russia will become more democratic while the west will become more socialistic."

* * *

Benjamin Franklin: "The man who empties his purse into his head is no fool."

* * *

Montaigne (1533-1592), French Humanist and essayist, in Little Blue Book 87: "Nothing is so firmly believed as what we know least." .... "Miracles are according to the ignorance wherein we are by nature, and not according to nature's essence."

* * *

George Moore, novelist: "There is not one atom of evidence of the existence of a good, wise, and all-powerful God."

* * *

Ovid: "Exile is death." Victor Hugo: "Exile is life."

* * *

Cassius V. Cook, secretary of a Los Angeles group of Freethinkers and Libertarians, writes that Walter E. Holloway, one of the most remarkable characters in the movement for freedom, died on May 26, 1946, at the age of 70. During all his adult life he marched in the advanced phalanx of progress. Always a daring and a prolific thinker, he was ordinarily far in advance of his time. Mr. Cook adds that Holloway was a master of the English language, and so great an orator as to be remembered wherever he spoke for the power and influence of his eloquence. His most prominent part in the Freethought field was as an independent lecturer, for years, in San Francisco. Here he established one of the most successful lectureships that was ever kept going on the Pacific coast. Holloway assiduously applied himself to scientific, Freethought, and Libertarian subjects. In 1930, he published privately his "Rubaiyat of Today," which certain competent critics con-

sider to be his greatest gift to posterity and that will some day bring well-deserved recognition. Mr. Cook writes: "Always Walter Holloway gave himself unstintingly to causes that contributed to progress in terms of the enlightenment of the mind. To the end he was indifferent to fame, to fortune, or to the cost to himself. Many will long hold him in grateful memory."

* * *

Mrs. Priscilla Prissy-Pratt was peeved because the Methodist Ladies Society hadn't invited her to go with them to the church picnic. On the morning of the outing, however, the picnickers relented and asked her to join them. "It's too late," Mrs. Prissy-Pratt snapped. "I've already prayed for rain."

* * *

From the Socialist Party's 1946 Congressional Platform: "The United Nations must be replaced by a Democratic World Government with every human being a citizen. To make this possible, the great powers must renounce national sovereignty. The U. S. must lead the peoples of the world in the bold experiment."

* * *

Real estate agent, to prospect in suburban Wichita: "Not only will you find the air out this way good, but you'll always be able to have more than you can use."

* * *

Traditional notice backstage at every vaudeville house: "Don't Send Out Your Laundry Until the Manager Has Seen Your Act."

* * *

Harold J. Laski, chairman, British Labor Party Executive Committee: "Our Labor government's policy for India might turn a lot of enemies into friends if only Churchill would stop talking."

* * *

Johnnie Best, Chicago, Ill.: "Here in Chicago, the well-regimented West Side Catholics are picketing the movie theater showing Howard Hughes' famous film, 'The Outlaw.' Priests of seven West Side churches blasted the film from their pulpits and they've promised to increase the picket line to 2,000 unless the management cuts certain scenes from the movie . 'The Outlaw' is nothing but a wholesome, six-gun, old-fashioned Western. But the picture serves as a medium for mass pressure on theater managers, thereby enabling the hierarchy to exercise an extra-legal censorship. Fanaticism and bigotry are on the march. The priests will not be satisfied until they have complete control of the movies, the radio and the press. Sex purity is merely a subterfuge. The real motive is political and social—to take over the means of communication and thereby take control of the mass mind."

* * *

Alexander Dumas, in Little Blue Book 66: "I prefer the wicked rather than the foolish. The wicked sometimes rest."

* * *

Zenobius: "He is either dead or teaching school."

* * *

George Herbert, in "Jacula Prudentum": "Religion can bear no jesting."

* * *

Israel Zangwill, in "Children c the Ghetto": "Let us start a nev religion with one commandant, 'En joy thyself.' "

* * *

Sir Thomas Browne, in "Hydri otaphia": "The religion of on seems madness unto another."

* * *

Josh Billings: "The mule is ha hoss and haf jackass, and thei kums a full stop, natur discoverin her mistake."

* * *

La Place, to Napoleon, when th latter asked why God wasn't mentioned in his book on astronomy: "Sire, I had no need for that hypothesis."

* * *

Montaigne, in Little Blue Book: "Man is certainly stark mad; he cannot make a flea, and yet he will be making gods by dozens."

* * *

Robert G. Ingersoll, in "Shakespeare": "There is the same difference between talent and genius that there is between a stone mason and a sculptor."

* * *

You were right in rejecting the ad that offers McCarthy's anti-Semitic book, even though it contains material in support of Freethought. Race-baiting is a form of mental disease and deserves no place among civilized people, though I regret to find that the cancer has spread to sections where one might at least hope that such bigotry would be erased. I am reminded of a statement made by David Lloyd George, in 1926, on the plight of the Jews. It seems to me that Lloyd George has summarized in a few sentences the absurdity of the whole case against a helpless minority. I suggest that you reprint it.

Lloyd George's characterization of anti-Semitism:

If the Jews are rich they are birds of prey. If they are poor they are vermin. If they are in favor of war it is because they want to exploit the bloody feuds of the Gentiles for their own profit. If they are anxious for peace they are instinctive cowards or traitors. If labor is oppressed by great capital, the greed of the Jew is held responsible. If labor revolts against capital, as it did in Russia, the Jew is blamed for that also. If he lives in a strange land, he must be persecuted and pogrommed out of it. If he wants to go back to his own he must be prevented.

* * *

CPSIA information can be obtained
at www.ICGtesting.com
Printed in the USA
BVHW041210281218
536599BV00014B/406/P